Self Manual

Valeria

Contents

Dedications

I dedicate this book to my mom and my father, whom I lost at a time when I did not fully understand their importance in my life.

I thought I could fly without you, but came to realise that in rejecting you, I was rejecting myself. I searched for you in others, losing my confidence and self-worth along the way.

I love you to the moon and back, and I know you live within me. I am eternally grateful for the life you gave me. Nothing else has any greater importance.

I dedicate this book to all the souls who, at some point in their lives, have felt lost and helpless. I have been there myself and wholeheartedly would like to convey one message to you - My dear reader, know that you are never alone, and you are stronger than you can imagine.

I'm also deeply grateful to the Gulf Publishing Team, who made this possible.

May this book serve as a guide to help you find your way back to yourself, to healing, and to wholeness.

Acknowledgements

I want to express my gratitude to my sister. Even though we may have disagreements and arguments, we always manage to reconnect with heartfelt messages after the storm has passed. I am thankful for my friends who accept me for who I am and encourage me to keep going, especially during times when I feel down. I also want to thank every person I tried to build a relationship with, but that didn't work out. You all inspired me to stop dwelling on "why" and instead start seeking answers to "what for?" and "what I can do." Looking back, I appreciate the way these experiences have shaped my personality and forced me to expand my narrow views.

About The Author

Valeria grew up in a small, remote village in Ukraine, raised by her hardworking mother alongside her sister. After her parents separated and her mother remarried, she felt a deep need for stability, leading her to leave home after finishing high school. Valeria first pursued an education in economics, graduating from the Ukrainian Odesa State College of Management and Trade. However, after facing the loss of her parents and suffering a stroke at 33, she turned to psychology for answers.

Valeria's personal struggles inspired her to dig deeper into self-development and healing. She went on to study psychology at the Ukrainian-Polish University of Central Europe, becoming a psychological consultant. She now works in luxury retail abroad and offers online psychological support to others in her spare time.

Her journey is one of resilience and growth, and she hopes her experiences can inspire others to find healing and peace in their own lives. Faith is now a big part of her story, which she plans to share in future books.

Introduction

It took me over 10 years to reach a point where I'm ready to share from my heart, drawing on my lived experiences and hardships through seeking answers, enduring breakdowns, recovering from a stroke, and navigating my broken heart multiple times.

I believe people don't delve into psychology unless they're facing significant challenges.

My humble hope is that you will find the book useful and helpful.

Thank you for your courage in embarking on this path of self-discovery and growth.

We all want to achieve happiness, and for each person, it means different things in life. For that reason, the book is called Self Manual. Your journey is unique, and no one else is walking in your shoes.

You might spend time listening to others' advice and comparing yourself and your life to others. Sometimes, you might feel sad or content in the process.

However, Comparison often leads to competition, fostering pride on one side and wretchedness on the other. Pride and wretchedness are two sides of the same coin.

My suggestion is to discard any scales of good or bad, any comparisons that breed internal conflicts. We know very well that two different people will do the same task differently.

Even siblings who grow up in the same household will have distinct memories and perceptions of their childhood experiences. These differences are shaped by their unique personalities, emotional responses, and the roles they played within the family.

Honouring these individual experiences starts with connecting deeply with ourselves. By understanding our own emotions, memories, and perspectives, we become better equipped to respect and appreciate the unique experiences of others. This self-awareness fosters empathy, allowing us to connect with others on a deeper level, acknowledging that their experiences, though different from ours, are equally valid and meaningful.

In today's world, we are bombarded with information and distractions, all vying for our attention. If we become wise consumers of information, we can benefit by taking only what we need. However, if we immerse ourselves in everything and try to be everywhere, we risk drifting farther and farther away from our true selves.

Here are a few aims why I wrote this manual:

1. To guide you on how to navigate your unique path, free from unnecessary comparisons and distractions, leading you closer to a balanced and authentic life.

2. To guide you to delve into personal introspection and understanding how our internal motivations and barriers impact various aspects of our lives, particularly concerning goals and relationships.

Throughout this book, I will be reminding you that self-control is great; self-awareness is the key. Ultimately, this book is your path to yourself and your uniqueness. My sincere intention in writing this book is for you to become curious about yourself and discover or rediscover yourself.

We say that every person is unique, yet we are influenced by the social aspect of success and fail to celebrate our uniqueness.

The quality of relationships with other people is a detailed model of attitude towards oneself. Other people reflect what is happening in us.

As humans, while we might be able to achieve personal goals and satisfy some emotional needs on our own, our survival and overall well-being as a species are inherently tied to forming relationships. Relationships—whether familial, work, friendly, or romantic—are crucial for our emotional support, growth, and even physical survival. This interconnectedness is what has allowed humans to thrive as a species, emphasising the importance of community and collaboration.

The respect we show others often mirrors the respect we have for ourselves. When we hold ourselves in high regard, understanding our own worth, boundaries, and values, it naturally extends to how we treat others. Conversely, if we struggle with self-respect, it can sometimes manifest in how we interact with and perceive others. This idea underscores the importance of self-awareness and self-compassion as foundations for building respectful, healthy relationships with others.

Have you ever wondered?

Why doesn't a person feel loved?

Even when love is shown. Believe me, someone always loves you. Why don't you feel it? The answer is that the feeling of being loved is proportional to what you have given to other people in the form of love.

The extent to which you are able to love another is the extent to which you are able to feel that you are loved.

By not loving others, we deprive ourselves of feeling love.

When can we love others? The answer is when we accept ourselves totally with all our flows. We can love, understand, and forgive another person to the extent that we love, understand, and forgive ourselves. No one is better, and no one is worse. Please remove this black-and-white thinking. Every human being who is walking on the earth has the right to exist exactly the way one does. If you do not understand something, it does not mean it has no right to exist.

The word acceptance entails not fighting mode but a peaceful one. I know it is deep, right, so reflect on it.

How often do you judge someone? We tend to judge; this way, it is easier than taking a moment to think about what circumstances led this person to the situation of being judged, assuming that we know everything better. I compel you to broaden your views.

How many times have you tried to change someone by imposing your life view? What did you get in return? Take a minute to reflect … how what you oppose in others related to you? What kind of truth you might ignore about yourself.

Fighting to be right can often lead to an aggressive approach where you feel as if the world is against you. This mindset can create walls between you and others, leading to isolation and a lack of genuine connections. When the focus shifts to winning an argument or proving a point, the essence of communication—understanding, empathy, and connection—is lost.

In such situations, the need to be right can overshadow the importance of relationships. It creates a defensive posture that pushes people away, making it difficult to form or maintain meaningful bonds. True connection requires openness, vulnerability, and the willingness to listen and understand, even when you don't agree. By letting go of the need to always be right, you can foster an environment where mutual respect and understanding thrive, paving the way for deeper, more fulfilling relationships.

Just as aggressively fighting to be right can isolate you, constantly adopting a victim mentality and submitting to others can be equally damaging. When you see yourself as a victim in every situation, you surrender your power and allow others to dictate your life. This can lead to feelings of helplessness, resentment, and a deep sense of misery.

This submissive approach often stems from a fear of conflict or a desire to avoid discomfort, but it ultimately robs you of your agency and self-worth. It can also create imbalanced relationships where your needs and boundaries are consistently overlooked, leading to a cycle of dissatisfaction and emotional exhaustion.

True happiness and fulfilment come from finding balance— asserting yourself when necessary, respecting your own boundaries, and engaging in relationships as an equal. It's about recognising that you have a voice and that your feelings and perspectives matter just as much as anyone else's. By stepping out of the victim role, you reclaim your power and open yourself up to more authentic, empowering connections.

Every relationship you are in and every goal you pursue share one common element: you. To have a good relationship with people means to undergo deep self-reflection and inner work. The same fashion applies to our goals we want to achieve in life.

No one stops us from doing what we want but ourselves.

We take ourselves everywhere we go, carrying the stories we hold inside us.

This manual aims to help you navigate your journey with self-love, acceptance, and forgiveness, fostering healthier relationships and a more authentic life.

We all desire a life that includes self-realisation and great relationships—the ones where we can trust, be ourselves, and navigate personal transformation and growth safely together. We tend to avoid pain in relationships, and it is the biggest issue that actually creates a scenario where changing partners, seeking happiness as if there is some perfect match, will magically change our life and our perception of life or save us from our life, failing.

We always receive what is right for us in every given moment, and we always have everything we need to go forward and better our lives.

Achieving harmony, although I do not fancy this term much, however, to have harmony in relationships and work requires our honesty with ourselves first.

I suggest you get to know yourself first, not place expectations on others and suffer afterwards because people cannot live up to your expectations or fulfil your needs just due to their own agenda.

Sometimes, we want them to play roles for us that they are not capable of, regardless of one's efforts. Moreover, there are only two people who love us unconditionally: our parents. And our connection with them, or lack of it, plays a crucial role in all our relationships.

Simply hoping for better won't work; what works is being honest with ourselves, being empathetic toward ourselves and taking responsibility for ourselves are signs of healing and maturing.

Dedicating ourselves to what we truly want and taking full responsibility for everything in our lives— the partner we complain about is our responsibility, our mirror, the job we hate is our responsibility and our choice, the way we feel, act, react is of our making that comes from within.

In this book, you will find your own answers—not unsolicited advice or clichéd positive speeches. You will receive the truth you are ready for, guiding you towards a more authentic and fulfilling life.

"He who looks outside dreams; he who looks inside, awakens." — Carl Jung

Remember, while self-control is a valuable sign of strength, self-awareness is the key.

This book is a guide for you to start understanding how your psyche works and to help you learn how to have a self-dialogue.

Do not wait until you have many relationships that end abruptly and painfully in similar scenarios.

If this has happened to you and you try to suppress your emotions and move on, please read this carefully now.

There is no mechanism in our psyche that allows us to switch on joy and positivity while switching off anger, sadness, helplessness, and despair. Our psyche switches everything off simultaneously. When this happens, joy ceases to be joy, love loses its essence, achievements feel empty, and everything becomes dull and meaningless.

Do not wait until you feel nothing at all.

Do not ignore yourself by repressing your feelings until your body metaphorically screams for help. Everything you need is inside you. What pains you will also cure and liberate you. This might sound bizarre now, but it is the truth.

Think about it for a moment: 95% of our behaviour is ruled by our unconscious mind. Our emotions and feelings are engines of action. When we do not understand them, our actions remain unconscious.

We all live in programs of the unconscious, and it is impossible to get clarity through our heads, only through our feelings. Knowledge and someone's advice do not work.

It is easy to say, but it is hard to do - this is when only knowledge-how is not enough.

It is worth deepening your knowledge about you.

In this book, I will suggest you ask yourself challenging questions and be honest with yourself—for your own sake, not for anyone else's.

Choosing to embark on this journey for yourself means you are committed to your own path, regardless of lack of applause or encouragement from others. In some cases, you may find yourself alone in this endeavour. Do it for yourself—this is the only way to steadily move forward, step by step.

Your life is your journey. You possess within you everything needed to achieve your desires.

Remember, while self-control is a valuable sign of your strength, self-awareness is the key.

How do you get there? By allowing yourself to feel all your feelings—every single one, without exception. This is the path to deep self-awareness and understanding.

This book will guide you through practices that transcend habitual thinking. These practices will lead you to explore all aspects of yourself within the contexts of relationships and personal goals, uncovering inner causes and understanding cause-effect connections.

I will highlight the benefits of reading this book and doing the outlined work:

Understanding Patterns: You will discover how you fall into particular patterns of thoughts and behaviours.

Emotional Regulation: You will learn how to self-regulate your emotions in the moment.

Accessing Hidden Resources: You will tap into your own hidden resources that were obscured by suppressed emotions.

Becoming Your Own Psychologist: You will develop the ability to self-assess and understand yourself better.

For example:

When feeling sad, instead of following the usual pattern of thoughts and behaviours, you will practice connecting with yourself, understanding why you feel this way and providing what you truly need.

When experiencing a strong reaction towards someone without a clear reason, you will explore the underlying reasons for this reaction.

If doubts arise about your goals despite all rational considerations being in place, you will have the tools to explore and understand these doubts.

You will acquire a toolkit of self-awareness practices.

Begin by setting your intentions and goals. Use a notebook to write down your feelings, changes and insights. Every day can bring a newness to your perspective and you will track your progress.

Define how you feel now and how you want to feel emotionally and physically after completing your work.

Identify specific relationships you want to focus on and heal.

List desires or wishes you've been delaying and create a plan for them.

Record your current thoughts about relationships and the thoughts you aim to cultivate.

- Outline the steps you intend to take to achieve your goals.

This process will help you start your journey towards self-awareness and personal growth.

There are important rules to follow here—be careful and gentle with yourself:

1. Step-by-Step Approach: Don't try to do all the practices at once. Take your time and proceed gradually.

2. Patience with Results: Avoid demanding immediate results from yourself. Give yourself the necessary time to process before moving on

3. Respect Your Energy Levels: Don't push yourself to practice when you're low on sleep or lacking energy. Stay in the process at your own pace.

4. Personal Commitment: Engage in this process for yourself, focusing on your own journey and well-being.

5. Natural Unfolding: Understand that your work on yourself will unfold slowly and steadily over time.

6. Give Yourself Time To Rest & Rejuvenate: Listen to your body's needs—whether it's eating, sleeping, or simply resting.

During your practice, either you write down answers or have self-dialogue, asking yourself suggested questions, and you may experience the release of tension and emotions. This might make you feel good, or it could bring up sadness. Remember, this is a normal part of the healing and transformation process of the psyche. Be kind and gentle with yourself as you navigate these changes.

By following these guidelines, you can nurture a supportive and compassionate environment for your personal growth and self-discovery journey.

You are holding this book. I applaud you. It is a courageous step that many will avoid doing.

Accumulated feelings may surface during this process, but they might not be directly related to the current moment. You may find yourself more sensitive and emotional for a while.

During this time:

Avoid Making Decisions: Refrain from making significant decisions for a few weeks or even a month. Your brain may try to rationalize what's happening, but your body is in the process of releasing long-held emotions.

Allow Feelings to Surface: It's important to let these feelings rise and live them out. Repressing pain only prolongs it. As the saying goes, "Who does not cry is prepared to cry forever."

Emotional Release: Living through these emotions is the only way to free your body from emotional blockages.

Inform Your Close Circle: Warn your close circle of friends and family about what you're going through. Let them know you may be more sensitive than usual, but reassure them that it's temporary.

Maintain Stability in Relationships: Avoid making radical decisions such as separations, divorces, or quitting jobs during this period. Emotions can be intense but temporary, and it's crucial not to jeopardize important relationships or stability.

By following these guidelines, you can navigate this period of emotional release with greater understanding and support, fostering healing and growth without unnecessary disruption to your life. I highly recommend incorporating physical activities like sports, yoga, and breathing exercises into your routine. A strong body has a greater capacity to process feelings, emotions, stress, and daily life challenges.

Additionally, prioritise regular physical checkups and proper nutrition to support your overall well-being.

The practices outlined in this book will require mental resources. By holding this book, you've shown readiness for this journey.

Working on yourself through these practices has the potential to transform how you interact with yourself and the world around you. Therefore, resistance may arise. You might find yourself hesitant to engage in the practices. Recognise this resistance when it appears and address it with understanding and determination. I believe in you—I've been through this journey myself, and I am now healing and reconnecting with myself. Actually, it is a lifetime journey. Once you pass one level after a while, you may encounter different feelings. But you should never think that there hasn't been any progress. Progress is always there.

My first revelation was when, after starting my journey of self-discovery, I became less judgemental toward people and less reactive. Yes, I felt negative about the actions of the person, but I could separate the action from the person and still remain calm and not super emotionally charged. So, my world became less black and white. There was less war and more acceptance. Why? I stopped thinking I was better or smarter; I was human too, and I might make the same mistakes as this person I had just judged.

To mind my own business was my decision.

Why? When you start to work with yourself, you start to value your energy and crave balance, and you are able to control it by choosing your fights carefully.

Perceive this journey as if you are embarking on an exploration of the home inside you. You're doing this for yourself—to create a sense of belonging in your own body.

I love the metaphor: ultimately, the goal is to become a cosy and welcoming home for yourself, embracing and accepting all parts of who you are. This journey is about nurturing a deep connection with yourself and finding comfort and peace within.

If you or your family have experienced any loss or tragedy in your life, I highly recommend working through it in therapy. This book will give you an understanding, but processes may be revealed that one way or another need to be carried into personal therapy. Trust me on this: we need professional support not because we cannot handle it but because we want to go to another level and feel better, subsequently, better.

Throughout this book you will have many deep, self-reflective practices intended to help you in area of relationships, suppressed emotions, work with inner child, personal goals, day to day awareness. While some practices can be done independently, there are others where professional support is invaluable. I highly recommend personal psychotherapy, as it can save a significant amount of time in one's life.

Chapter 1:
Our Amazing Psyche

Our psyche will hide overwhelming emotions to protect us, but in doing so, it also hides our true nature, which encompasses courage, healthy aggression, self-worth, joy, contempt, talents, self-love, self-respect, compassion, and empathy.

What I mean here is that when emotions are suppressed rather than acknowledged and validated, we expend a great deal of our mental and vital energy to keep them suppressed. It creates internal conflicts, and this effort pushes away something truly ours—our natural identity. Meanwhile, our stubborn psyche desires this energy and our true nature back, leading to repeated scenarios until we get it.

Over 100 years ago, Freud described this process as the repetition or reconstruction of trauma. The psyche attracts similar experiences in an attempt to finally find a solution, heal, and integrate these experiences. Only then can we truly move forward and create new experiences.

Human nature is vulnerable, yet our psyche strives for healing and integrity.

Deep-seated, default-mode beliefs often originate from childhood. Freud referred to this as the Achilles heel in human development. During this period, our analytical part—the neocortex—and our limbic brain are not yet fully developed.

Without a self-sufficient brain to see the bigger picture, analyze events, and separate ourselves from others, all emotions during childhood can feel overwhelming, almost as if they are life-or-death experiences.

There is also a distinction between psychological age and physical age. Physical age is merely a number according to your passport, while emotional or psychological age can differ significantly.

Although we may physically age year by year, this does not mean that we progress emotionally at the same pace. Psychological stuckness can occur due to traumatic events—such as separation from family, early separation from mom, emotionally absent parents, parental divorce, personal divorce, death of a loved one, suicide attempts, developmental trauma, which I call the trauma of love, betrayal, loss of job, any sudden, intense, and isolated event. These experiences live in our bodies and leave lasting echoes in our lives, impacting us profoundly. Nothing leaves us without a trace.

We may live as fully-fledged adults in one area of our lives while in another area, we may react and behave as if we are 3, 7, or 13 years old, reflecting the age at which our psyche got stuck due to a particular experience. For instance, we might be high achievers at work but avoid the area of relationships as a protective, compensatory strategy—or vice versa, focusing on relationships to avoid social or professional challenges.

We are all influenced by our traumatic experiences—there are no exceptions. Some may be affected more intensely than others, but these experiences shape us all. Just as we drive a car automatically, we often react to situations and fall into patterns of behaviour automatically as well. The psyche tries to preserve itself in a stressful situation and "splits off" the traumatised part. The experience is activated unconsciously, remains relevant and becomes available at each encounter with a trigger. At the same time, a person regresses to the age and situation where the traumatization occurred, and at these moments.

Chapter 2:
Why We Need To Work With Our Feelings?

The impact of a traumatic experience isn't solely the event itself but the unprocessed emotions that linger within us. These unexpressed or unresolved emotions can create deep psychological and even physical imprints, influencing how we perceive ourselves, others, and the world around us.

When emotions like fear, anger, or grief remain unaddressed, they can manifest as ongoing pain, unhealthy behaviour patterns, or emotional numbness, which may affect relationships, self-esteem, and overall well-being. Processing these emotions is key to healing and reclaiming a sense of balance and peace.

First Reason:

By suppressing our feelings, we inadvertently prolong them. Those who do not allow themselves to cry may find themselves prepared to cry forever. When people do not have a safe relationship with their emotional experiences, this can stop them from feeling and integrating the emotions. Emotions that are not felt and experienced naturally will manifest through other means of expression.

The Second Reason:

Simultaneously with suppressed feelings, survival programs are formed—adaptive strategies, behaviours, avoidance, compensatory strategies and attitudes towards ourselves and the world. These include beliefs such as "I am not good enough," "I do not deserve," "I cannot do it," or "I have to deserve love, no one likes me, loves me, cares for me, I have to have 5 diplomas then I am ok otherwise I am a loser or stuff like that.

The Third Reason:

Transformation of the psyche begins when we engage with all our emotions and feelings, listen to our bodies, validate our feelings, and recognise our needs. Through these practices, you will embark on a journey of self-discovery and growth. You will learn how to ask yourself questions, and the answers will arrive not like words but like feelings or images. You will start to understand yourself better and learn to rely on yourself.

The Fourth Reason:

Recognising and working with our suppressed feelings is crucial for understanding ourselves and breaking free from these limiting patterns. It's a journey toward self-acceptance and authenticity.

The Fifth Reason:

Unresolved emotions have an impact on the body. Everything that remains incomplete or unresolved in your life—whether emotions, thoughts, or actions—gets stored in your physical body. This stored energy can manifest in various forms, drawing your energy away from other activities and impacting your overall well-being.

For example, something heavy is bothering you, and you have no energy to do what you wish, fall into a mode of procrastinating or distracting yourself, comforting through binge eating or TV watching while you are doing it, it seems ok, but it is time of your life passing away and brings no change and some of the worst regrets.

Unresolved issues often manifest as physical symptoms such as tension, pain, or chronic health conditions. The following symptoms can be seen as the body's way of signalling that there are underlying issues needing attention:

Energy Drain:

Incomplete emotional processes or unresolved conflicts draw a significant amount of your energy. This can lead to feelings of fatigue, stress, and a general sense of being overwhelmed.

Here's how it unfolds: emotions are released and form into stronger feelings. These feelings shape our experiences, which in turn create belief systems and convictions. These convictions then manifest in our actions, establishing patterns of behaviour that may act as blind spots, hindering us from achieving our true desires. When we seek constant approval and authority, it indicates a trauma of rejection.

For Example: The need to please others often stems from a desire to control their opinions, fearing that without their approval, we cannot accept our true selves. This fear can feel overwhelming, metaphorically suffocating us as we try to keep our emotions buried.

When you feel the need for everyone to like you, it's important to pause and ask yourself a few deep questions to uncover what's truly driving this desire:

Why do you need it?

What is motivating this need for approval? Is it rooted in a fear of rejection, a desire for validation, or a longing to belong?

1. What part of you needs it?

Is there a part of your past or an unresolved emotional wound that craves acceptance and affirmation from others?

2. What is the true need?

Is the need for external validation masking a deeper need for self-acceptance, self-worth, or inner peace?

3. What will happen if no one likes you?

Imagine the scenario where you don't receive the approval you're seeking. What emotions come up? What do you fear will happen?

4. What is the worst that could happen?

By confronting the worst-case scenario, you can start to dismantle the irrational fears and anxieties that might be driving your behaviour.

When you ask these questions, you begin to uncover your deeper fears—fears that might be influencing your actions and decisions. By understanding these fears, your subconscious can start to provide answers and clarity, helping you differentiate between the present and the past. You can remind yourself that this is a different time, and everything is different now.

This process allows you to separate past experiences from your current reality. It empowers you to approach situations with a clearer perspective, freeing yourself from the compulsion to be liked by everyone. Instead, you can focus on being authentic, knowing that true self-worth comes from within, not from the approval of others.

Example: Imagine you struggle to express your love honestly to your partner, fearing rejection. This reluctance reveals a vulnerability rooted in past hurts that continue to influence your current relationships.

Taking back your emotional investments—your dreams, plans, and the energy you've poured into them—can be a powerful act of self-reclamation. Here's how you might approach this process:

Acknowledge Your Investments

Recognise where you've poured your emotional energy—whether it's into relationships, dreams, or plans that haven't panned out as you hoped. Acknowledge the time, love, and effort you've invested.

1. Identify What No Longer Serves You

Reflect on which of these emotional investments are no longer serving you or contributing to your growth and well-being. It might be an unfulfilled dream, a relationship that drains you, or a plan that feels stagnant.

2. Release Attachments

Allow yourself to let go of these attachments. This doesn't mean abandoning your dreams or plans entirely but rather releasing the emotional hold they have on you. Free yourself from the need for specific outcomes.

3. Reclaim Your Energy

Visualise gathering back all the energy you've invested in these areas. Imagine it returning to you, revitalizing your spirit and restoring your inner strength. This energy is yours to redirect wherever you choose.

4. Refocus on the Present.

Shift your focus to the present moment. Consider what truly aligns with your current self and where you want to channel your reclaimed energy. This could mean setting new goals, nurturing yourself, or simply being more present.

5. Rebuild with Intention.

With your energy back in your control, rebuild your dreams and plans with intention. Ensure that they align with your true desires and current reality rather than past expectations or external pressures.

6. Practice Self-Compassion.

Be gentle with yourself throughout this process. It's okay to grieve the loss of what you hoped for, but remember that reclaiming your energy is an act of self-love and empowerment.

By taking back your emotional investments, you regain control over your life and choices. You're not abandoning your dreams or plans but rather reshaping them to better serve your growth and happiness. This process allows you to move forward with renewed energy and a clearer sense of purpose.

Example: Consider wanting to address your boss about their passive-aggressive communication style but fearing repercussions. This fear doesn't represent your entire self; it reflects a scared inner part.

Consequently, you may remain silent, lose sleep, become irritable with your family, or even direct aggression towards yourself.

When you feel fear in a situation or in the presence of someone, it's important to explore the roots of that fear and address it:

1. What part of you is scared?

Identify the aspect of yourself that feels fear. Is it a vulnerable, childlike part of you that feels unsafe? Or is it a part of you that has been hurt in similar situations before? Understanding which part of you is scared can help you address the fear more effectively.

2. Whom do you unconsciously see in this person?

Sometimes, fear arises because we unconsciously project past experiences onto a current situation. Ask yourself if this person reminds you of someone from your past—a parent, a former partner, or someone who once hurt you. Recognizing this can help you separate the past from the present.

3. Release your own anger.

If there's anger connected to this fear, allow yourself to acknowledge and release it. This could be anger at yourself for feeling vulnerable or anger towards someone who has hurt you before. Allow this anger to surface without judgment, and find a healthy way to express it—whether through writing, talking to someone, or physical activity.

4. Give yourself permission to fully experience your emotions.

Don't suppress them or rush through them. Whether it's crying, screaming, or simply sitting with your feelings, let them flow naturally.

5. Address your anger.

Once you've allowed the anger to surface, address it directly. Ask yourself what this anger is telling you. Is it a sign that your boundaries have been crossed? Or is it revealing a deeper hurt that needs healing?

Understanding the root of your anger helps you process it more effectively.

6. Give the part of yourself that's scared all the energy you can.

Direct your energy towards the part of you that feels scared. Reassure this part of you that it's safe, that you are in control now. Speak to yourself with kindness and compassion, offering the support you might have needed in the past but didn't receive.

7. You grow stronger within.

As you go through this process, you'll find that you become stronger. By facing your fear, acknowledging your anger, and nurturing the part of you that feels scared, you build inner resilience. This strength allows you to move forward with greater confidence and emotional clarity.

Through this inner work, you transform fear into strength and anger into empowerment, allowing you to navigate life's challenges with a stronger, more balanced sense of self.

What impedes our ability to change often lies deep within us, originating from earlier experiences that may be difficult to recall.

Chapter 3:
Childhood

Before you proceed to the next chapter, let me tell you my story so you might relate to the coping strategies you could have developed over the years that keep you from getting what you long for deep inside.

I understood one thing clearly: in order to move forward, we have to revisit and acknowledge past experiences and honour them. Once we do that, only then these past experiences will stop governing our future decisions and the way we see the world and those around us.

I grew up in a tiny village so remote you'd need a satellite to find it—Google Maps won't even register it. I was surrounded by two beautiful women- my sister and my mom. Our house had its quirks—one of the walls kept falling, and the front door always seemed to have issues. You can guess there was no male figure around to fix it. My mom raised us on her own, facing every challenge with strength and resilience.

Before my parents officially divorced, they were already living apart. My father would visit from time to time, but everything changed when my mom remarried and started a new family with my beautiful younger sister. I felt out of place, longing for a quieter, more stable household. In those moments, my friend's family became my family, offering me the sense of belonging I was searching for.

I grew up protective of my mom, rejecting my father, and fearing my stepfather.

I felt responsible for every person in my family older than me. It was too much for a child to carry. After finishing high school, I left and never came back home.

I wanted to build something of my own, not be entangled in a family drama. My father died when I was 19, and my mom when I was 30.

I had grown accustomed to living without them, yet whatever we bury within ourselves eventually comes back to confront us. I missed them when they were alive, and when they were gone, I tried to numb the pain—but it lingered.

Despite everything, I did quite well for myself. I found a job abroad and quickly knew that I was meant to live outside my homeland.

At 33, I had a stroke. Recovering took time, and I realised that something had to change. My anxiety felt constant; Small tasks would make me worry that something could go wrong. I feared losing control or depending on anyone. I was too sensitive, and it was wearing me off.

That's when my interest in psychology began.

I started with self-help books, but they didn't change how I felt. My head was filled with stories, examples, and information I could understand and could not apply. I thought one thing and ended up doing a different thing, further losing respect for myself. It was happening because I kept hiding the true suppressed emotions inside me, trying to keep up with logical approaches.

Then, I took self-development courses, which brought even more heavy emotions to the surface. I came to realise that I can not simply ask for what I want. If I could not identify my needs in relationships, I would long for a complete merger with no personal boundaries established, disrespecting another person's boundaries just because I had no boundaries of my own.

Finally, I pursued formal education as a psychological consultant and attended two professional schools of family counsellations. I studied the psyche and how developmental trauma affects the brain and human experience.

I had no idea how much this early experience affected me and shaped my following decisions until later, when I confronted it in personal therapy. I had to come back to my feelings—15-20 years old— that shaped my perception of life and people in order to make changes in the way I feel on a daily basis.

It was there that I started to understand why I felt the way I did and the reasons behind the choices I made.

What truly moved me and led to real change was honouring my past, working with my suppressed feelings in personal therapy, and building compensatory relationships with professionals to learn how to trust and feel valid.

My first coping strategy was to protect the weaker party in the name of justice, rebelling against those I saw as wrong. As it appeared later, I was unconsciously projecting my own inner scared part on those I tried to help or defend.

My second strategy was to escape anything that required patience, resolution, submission to hierarchy, or tolerating uncertainty. Having grown up on my own, I had issues with trusting people. Running was a default strategy, just like I ran from home as a teenager. My pattern was of either becoming co-dependent or developing deep resentment in relationships, which stemmed from unresolved childhood trauma around love and attachment.

As I pointed out earlier, part of us carries the inner child into adulthood, particularly the wounded aspects. These unresolved wounds can manifest as co-dependency—where the individual seeks constant validation or approval—or resentment, where there's emotional withdrawal and distrust in love.

Frankly, deep inside, I felt so unsafe, so the best-case scenario for me, I am joking, of course, now, would be to isolate myself.

My feeling was that I was not okay, that people were not okay, and that the world around me was not to be trusted.

These strategies, born from a small, fearful part of me, worked for a while—until they didn't. I realised something was wrong. My thoughts were distorted, and my reality was a direct consequence of them. I came to understand that our suppressed, unacknowledged, unhealed feelings precede our thoughts and actions.

I feared uncertainty, and it seemed like the ocean of loneliness was inside me. Naturally, it was exhausting. Back then, I did not realise cutting my connection with my roots and family. I was farther and farther away from me, and the anxiety took a toll on me.

Maybe if I had stayed in that tiny village, I wouldn't have changed. But the bigger world demanded something different from me, pushing me to evolve, adapt, and confront the truth about it, which I may have never faced otherwise.

How can someone live in a world where uncertainty and change are constants? I would have needed to isolate myself from everyone and everything; obviously, this would not have helped me at all.

And what about earning money, obtaining a job, building relationships, and making friends? Could I really leave everything up to chance? These were the questions that plagued me.

Plus, my inner wounded child kept on seeking support and validation. This alone made all my relationships go in the wrong direction.

This was and is my journey and the reason I uncovered these truths for myself and decided to do something about it.

The differences between animal and human development are profound. While animal offspring quickly gain independence, human babies require approximately 18 years before leaving home and becoming self-sufficient adults. During this crucial developmental period, a human baby needs parental love, emotional closeness, and a safe environment that prioritizes their needs.

This foundational psychological condition is paramount for ensuring mental health and success in life. If parents are unable to provide this due to their own unresolved traumas, the child may struggle with chronic stress and anxiety, perceiving the world as unsafe. Conditional parental love can lead a child to strive excessively for approval, believing their survival depends on earning love.

Children who experience love trauma often find it difficult to leave unhealthy relationships, even when detrimental, because being with someone feels safer than being alone. They unconsciously seek to recreate a family dynamic they lacked in childhood, often sacrificing their well-being in the process. The fear of loneliness becomes unbearable, driving them to cling to relationships even if they are damaging.

People may struggle to let go and move on from relationships, indicating a deep-seated need for love and attention that wasn't fulfilled in childhood. Simple reason - you cannot leave your partner if unconsciously you place in him or her mom or father- not getting enough of them in childhood- then in exchange for any good word, some crumbs of attention and love, you will be ready to tolerate unhealthy relationships. A child who did not get enough parental love will have a hard time emotionally separating from their parents, going to one life as if still a baby, and it will only get more emotional over time without realizing it.

Questions like - who is inside me holding on to this relationship and this connection so much, and what is the true need? Trust your inner voice; it will bring new insights and clear thoughts. It is essential to understand how our unconscious works and separate partners from parental figures we might project on them.

No one ever can replace them, and no one ever can give enough to your inner child to fill the void, but you do. Your awareness of your story is crucial.

It is your responsibility. If you seek someone who will make decisions for you and care unconditionally, then you do not seek a partner; you seek a parental figure. It is not your fault, no one's fault. It is yours to take care of if you wish differently. Self-awareness is the key to a subsequent change. Conversely, some individuals may avoid closeness and relationships altogether, fearing that those they love will inevitably hurt them.

Unhealthy relationship dynamics, such as codependency and manipulation, often trace their roots back to childhood relationships with parents. Individuals unknowingly replicate these early dynamics with partners, friends, colleagues, and even bosses, perpetuating similar patterns of behaviour and emotional responses.

Understanding these dynamics is essential for breaking the cycle. It involves recognizing how childhood experiences shape adult relationships and working towards healing and establishing healthier patterns of connection and communication.

It took me years to understand why I kept losing myself in relationships, getting hurt, and then avoiding relationships altogether to avoid further pain. It took me years to realize how rejecting my parents affected me profoundly, leaving home when I was 13 years old and swearing never to come back and create a life and relationships that were completely different from my parent's life and relationships.

Looking back, I am amazed at how the trauma of rejection manifested in my personal relationships and work relationships, too. Not accepting my parents as an authority, I ended up unconsciously resisting bosses, too.

If you have such trauma, I want you to realise one thing: it will not go away even if you recognise it. You will need professional assistance and a secure bond with your therapist to give you a nonjudgmental space to heal it.

I sought answers in numerous self-help books.

I thought everyone got it but me.

Eventually, my frustration and anger drove me deeper into understanding myself, leading me to pursue an education and become a psychologist. I thought something was profoundly wrong with me.

What else can it be?

In psychology, it's recognised that within each of us reside various sub-personalities—such as the inner child, an adult part, and a parent. This concept was introduced by the Italian doctor and psychologist Roberto Assagioli within the psychotherapeutic system.

The primary goal of understanding sub-personalities is not to fight against or deny any part of ourselves nor to strive for an idealised personality. Such attempts would only lead to creating a false self, exacerbating inner conflicts, frustration, and, ultimately, self-betrayal. Accept all parts of oneself, even if they are contradictory! It is the key to inner freedom as a benefit that is released hidden within resources!

Different subpersonalities coexist in each of us, basic ones - child part, adult part, parental part- and there are more fascinating sub-personalities within us. It is important to take an inventory of which of them dominates in professional life and relationships and who is in charge of decision-making.

Connecting with your body, its feelings, and images is crucial because images are the language of our subconscious mind. Images are a direct pathway to accessing and understanding deeper layers of our psyche.

When we say, "I am collecting myself back" or "I feel like I'm in pieces," it reflects how our psyche can split into different parts:

- The part that recognises a situation has ended
- The part filled with unresolved emotions.
- The part unaware that the situation has ended.

These parts of you will be triggered in the future until you acknowledge it and give all your feelings the light of the truth.

Once you explore and acknowledge different parts of yourself, allowing each part to express its feelings without judgment or evaluation and identify its true needs, you begin to integrate these aspects of your psyche naturally. This process leads to changes in your adaptive strategies without needing extra effort or extensive self-education.

Each internal part represents a portion of our energy and vitality. When we integrate and activate all these parts, we effectively harness our energy and strength. Instead of creating internal disharmony, our energy begins to work in harmony, supporting our overall well-being.

This holistic approach to understanding and integrating our internal dynamics leads to greater inner peace, coherence, and a more balanced sense of self. Acceptance, truth, and experiencing all your feelings without any exceptions are keys to inner freedom.

Chapter 4:
Inner Child

The inner child is a part of us that remains unseen to others but accompanies us throughout our lives. Unlike physical toys that change over time, our inner child persists into adulthood, playing a vital role in our psyche.

The inner child is our desire to live, to want, to play, to explore, - it is a source of vitality, joy, and spontaneity. It embodies qualities like trust, gratitude, creativity, and a willingness to explore new experiences and connect with life. This aspect of ourselves is constantly seeking something—whether it's love, fulfilment, or self-expression.

If people find themselves disconnected from wanting anything or exploring, especially when they cannot play with their own children, this condition can be addressed by connecting to the inner child.

It's important to recognise that you are solely responsible for accessing and nurturing this part of your psyche—no one else can do it for you.

The feelings and moods of our inner child significantly influence how we perceive ourselves and experience daily life. They can manifest as feelings of trust, fear, anger, anxiety, sadness, apathy, or helplessness, impacting our emotional landscape profoundly.

Understanding and accepting our inner child is essential for cultivating self-awareness and emotional balance. By acknowledging its presence and nurturing its needs with compassion and care, we can heal past wounds, embrace our authentic selves, and foster a deeper sense of connection and joy in life.

Now, let's delve into how the inner child relates to your money, social relationships, and overall life satisfaction. The inner child's influence is profound and pervasive:

1. Money: The inner child's emotions and beliefs about worthiness, security, and abundance can impact your financial decisions and relationship with money. For example, feelings of scarcity or unworthiness may lead to self-sabotaging behaviours or difficulty in attracting prosperity.

2. Social Relationships: Your inner child's unresolved feelings and needs can affect how you relate to others. Issues like trust, fear of rejection, or difficulty in expressing yourself authentically may hinder your ability to form healthy, fulfilling relationships.

3. Life Fulfillment: The inner child plays a crucial role in your overall satisfaction with life. When this part feels neglected or unheard, it can manifest as a lack of joy, creativity, or enthusiasm for new experiences and opportunities for growth.

In close relationships, especially with those whose love and approval matter to you, your inner child's feelings often come to the forefront. Difficulties in expressing your needs, asserting boundaries, or embracing new challenges can all stem from unresolved childhood experiences that influence your present behaviour.

Addressing and healing the inner child involves nurturing and integrating these aspects of yourself. By fostering a compassionate relationship with your inner child, you can heal past wounds, reclaim your vitality and creativity, and ultimately enhance your ability to experience fulfilment and satisfaction in all areas of life.

Working with our feelings is essential because they reflect the state of our inner child. Feelings are complex and integral to our inner world. When we suppress or ignore them, we disconnect from ourselves and lose touch with our true emotions. This leads to inner conflict where we feel one thing, say another, and act differently altogether.

This pattern erodes self-trust and diminishes our inner confidence or sense of stability. We may hesitate to start new endeavours or doubt our capabilities, lacking belief in ourselves.

However, when we begin to engage with and process our feelings, our quality of life can improve dramatically. Awareness and connection with our inner parts allow us to understand our personal needs better. This process naturally activates the adult part of our psyche, bringing clarity and organization to our internal system.

As a result, we stop unconsciously seeking parental figures in our partners, spouses, bosses, or friends.

We're less likely to enter abusive or codependent relationships because we can meet our own needs. With self-awareness, we communicate more effectively and assertively, fostering healthier relationships based on mutual respect and understanding.

This doesn't mean we no longer need others to support us—it means we become more autonomous while still valuing and nurturing our connections with others. Ultimately, this shift leads to a higher quality of relationships and a greater sense of fulfilment in our lives.

Meeting Your Inner Child

Set an intention now to sort out within your inner world some feelings and emotions that you often have toward yourself, people, and life generally.

This practice aims to help you reconnect with your inner self, acknowledge past strategies, and empower you to make positive changes in your life. Embrace this process with patience and self-compassion, allowing yourself to heal and grow.

Let go of the need to control and analyse everything, and instead, listen to your heart and body. Sometimes, understanding feelings isn't about intellectualizing them but about experiencing them fully. Embrace the journey of connecting with your emotions without the pressure to dissect or rationalize them. This approach can lead to deeper self-awareness and emotional healing.

You can read it first and then do it on your own again and again until you master your self-dialogue.

Find a comfortable place and position for your body. Set an intention to relax completely. Begin by taking deep breaths—inhale deeply and exhale slowly. Breathe in… and breathe out. You can put on calming music to help your parasympathetic system kick in.

Feel your body relaxing as you focus on your head, forehead, eyes, and face. Relax your shoulders and neck, and allow your whole body to settle into a state of peace. If there's any tension present, acknowledge it without resisting. You might say to yourself, "I acknowledge my desire to control. It helps me feel safe, but right now, I can let go of control and trust in safety."

Feel a warmth spreading inside you, soothing away any remaining tension. Recognise that your body has its own innate ability to heal and restore itself. Embrace this wisdom and surrender to it. You are safe.

Detach yourself from the events and conversations of the day. Let go of the need to understand or explain things and release any expectations about how you should feel. Imagine your thoughts passing like clouds in the sky—drifting away peacefully.

Allow yourself to remain in this relaxed state for a moment, soaking in the calmness and serenity. Trust in the process of letting go and experiencing inner peace.

Now that you have accessed your inner world and connected with your inner feelings, it's time to pay attention to who is inside you right now and needs your attention.

Approach the process with openness and readiness to understand.

Ask yourself - Who is inside me needs my attention?

If you encounter a happy, younger part of yourself, embrace this moment with joy. Engage with this inner child, asking gently, "What do you want? How can I make you happy, happier?" Children often desire simple pleasures like ice cream, playtime, hugs, or attention. Keep asking until you uncover a genuine desire that brings joy to your inner child.

Engage in activities that nurture this vitality and joy—play, draw, dance—anything that resonates with this youthful energy. Recognise that this joyous and vibrant part is you. Embrace yourself with a hug, acknowledging and accepting this inner aspect of you.

Remember, your brain cannot differentiate between reality and imagination. Allow yourself to explore memories of your childhood—your talents, dreams, and what brought you happiness. Trust your unconscious to guide you as you listen deeply to what emerges.

Ask yourself what you wish to reintegrate into your life from these insights. This process allows you to reconnect with parts of yourself that may have been neglected or forgotten, fostering a deeper understanding and acceptance of your whole self.

Take your time to explore and connect with your inner world. If you don't immediately sense anything, that's okay. You can gently inquire within:

- Reflect on what emotions might be creating this sense of emptiness or sadness
- Allow yourself to acknowledge and accept it, allowing it to reveal its true nature.

What does it mean for you? What does it protect you from?

- Stay present with yourself, welcoming any sensations in your body as they arise.
- Remember, it's a process—don't rush or push yourself.
- Offer yourself love and acceptance throughout this exploration.

Remind yourself that by acknowledging and accepting all your feelings or lack thereof, you're creating space for healing and growth.

Do not fight or deny anything - once we deny something, it persists. Trust that everything will unfold in its own time when you're ready.

You can ask gently what it is you can not feel, or your resistance does not let you see?

If sadness arises or you feel like crying, embrace it as a sign of hidden emotions releasing and freeing up your energy. Allow yourself to experience and process these feelings with kindness and compassion toward yourself.

Thank yourself for your courage and commitment to this journey of self-discovery and healing. You're creating a safe space within yourself to connect deeply with your emotions and inner experiences.

Embracing this compassionate approach can lead to transformation and integration within yourself.

Part of your energy is stuck there with suppressed feelings, and you can release this energy by letting feelings flow. This practice fosters a deeper connection with yourself and encourages inner harmony and acceptance. It allows you to integrate all aspects of yourself, fostering healing and growth in your journey.

Allowing yourself to feel deeply and explore these inner dynamics is a courageous step towards healing.

Take a moment to breathe deeply and acknowledge the courage it takes to delve into these feelings. If you need a break at any point, an honour that you need and take the time you require.

If you encounter an image or feeling that initially feels negative:

- Emphasise that you won't try to change this part of yourself. It's important just as it is. By offering this unconditional acceptance and trust, you'll notice how these images or feelings begin to shift and evolve into something different. Welcome your feelings and validate their importance as part of your whole self. Embrace them fully, giving them the space they need without denial, repression, or avoidance.

Remember, it is your energy in the form of feelings.

- Express your desire to understand and accept this aspect of yourself fully.

Reassure this part of yourself

you care deeply about yourself.

You can say to your inner child - I found you! I see you! I will be here with you, and I will not leave you! I hold you.

Notice the feelings that arise as you connect with this younger part of yourself. If any judgment or resistance surfaces towards your inner child, reflect on whose perspective you might be seeing through. Whose eyes are judging or rejecting this part of you? Consider where you learned these critical thoughts or behaviours—perhaps from a parental figure or another significant person in your life.

It's important to recognise that those who may have hurt or misunderstood you did so because they themselves were hurt or lacked understanding toward themselves. Often, these patterns of behaviour are passed down through generations, unconsciously perpetuated until someone breaks the cycle.

By acknowledging this pattern, you can begin to heal and transform it within yourself. Approach this process with compassion and understanding for both yourself and those who influenced you. Through this awareness, you can learn to love and accept yourself in ways that may not have been modelled for you before.

It's crucial not to suppress any of your emotions. Accepting yourself fully and honouring all parts of your experience is a powerful step towards healing:

Now, as an adult, you have the strength and capacity to face and embrace these emotions. You can create a safe space within yourself to allow these feelings to flow freely. Visualize surrounding your inner child with warmth, support, love, and safety—imagine giving yourself comforting hugs in your inner world. You have the ability to provide all the care and compassion you needed back then. Do it now to support your inner child

You will feel the need to express your emotions. Imagine releasing them powerfully—perhaps through visualising rain, a thunderstorm, lightning, or even an earthquake. Allow yourself to scream, yell, or express your anger towards anyone or anything that has contributed to these feelings. Remember, all your feelings are valid and reasonable, and you have every right to feel what you are feeling. It's natural to love those who have cared for us while also feeling anger towards them at times. Embracing and allowing these conflicting feelings to coexist within us is a sign of your humanity and emotional richness. Your body is ready to release these emotions that it has been holding on to. Give space and recognise all the feelings. You can say it out loud.

Give a space to all feelings. Allow yourself to feel all your feelings

By acknowledging and accepting all your feelings, even if they seem contradictory, you can begin to resolve inner conflicts and find greater peace within yourself. Trust that it is safe to let these emotions flow— they are an essential part of your healing journey.

Here's the next guided practice to explore the decisions and strategies you've been living by:

Imagine yourself talking to your inner child. Ask yourself, "What decisions did You make about yourself, the world, and people back then?" Listen to the Answers

Praise, always praise your inner baby.

Be open and receptive to whatever comes up. Your inner child might bring forth memories, interactions, images, or spoken words. Trust what arises from within rather than from your rational mind.

Reflect on Your Strategies: Realise the strategies you developed to cope and survive. Acknowledge how these strategies helped you feel safe and protected.

Admit and Accept Change: Now, admit to yourself that you have the capacity to do things differently. Affirm that making changes will be safe and beneficial for you now.

Visualise Your Emotional Investment: Imagine the energy and emotional investment you've put into these strategies over the years. Picture this energy as a tangible form—whether it's fire, a cloud of energy, or a golden light.

Reclaim Your Energy: With your imagination, see this energy returning to you. Visualise it slowly entering your body, starting from the top of your head and spreading throughout every part of your body.

Feel the Healing: As this energy returns, feel it, bringing light, strength, and joy to every cell of your body. Notice any sensations you experience—warmth, tingling, waves of energy.

Accept the New Energy: Acknowledge and accept all the newfound strength and resources within you. Welcome them with gratitude for their healing power.

Capture Your Insights: Remember how your body feels now. Pay attention to any desires or needs that arise within you. What new decisions, ideas, or desires are emerging?

Take a moment to write down these insights. Note down what you wish to do differently moving forward, the new decisions you want to make, and any ideas or desires that surfaced during this practice.

Please give your inner child a good space in your body. Put a hand there; it can be your heart.

You can proclaim to yourself, "Everything you need, I will give it to you myself. You are inside me; you are safe and loved unconditionally."

Catharsis will not be enough. Remember, as an adult, you make a conscious decision to take care of your inner child and come up with real changes. You have uncovered recourses within you to make those changes.

To make you even stronger, this exercise allows you to reconnect with parts of yourself that may have been suppressed or forgotten, promoting healing and self-integration. Embrace the process with patience and openness, knowing that you are reclaiming your inner strength and authenticity.

Here's a next guided practice to help you reclaim and integrate parts of yourself that you may have pushed away or forgotten:

Set Your Intention: Intend to reconnect with parts of yourself that you may have lost or pushed away in the past experience. Affirm that you are ready to welcome back any qualities or aspects of yourself that need to return for your healing and wholeness.

Reflect on What You Gave Up: Ask yourself, "What did I give up there? What parts of me did I leave behind?" Allow your subconscious to bring forth any images, memories, or feelings associated with these lost parts.

Call It Back: Visualise or imagine these qualities or parts of yourself as a tangible form—an image, a feeling, or even a symbol. Say aloud or in your mind, "I need you back. You are important to me. Come back to me now."

Embrace What Returns: Notice what comes up. It could be a quality like strength, self-respect, healthy aggression, a carefree aspect of yourself, or a sexy, playful, joyous part of you. Welcome it back with open arms and a sense of gratitude.

Feel the Integration: As you welcome these parts back, feel a sense of warmth, joy, and wholeness within you. Acknowledge that integrating these parts is a natural and harmonious process.

Own Your Wholeness: Recognise that you are now more complete and integrated. Embrace all parts of yourself—as they are, they contribute to your inner harmony and well-being. Do not deny anything in yourself. What you deny or run from in you will persist. Give it a place inside you. By not excluding it, you heal yourself.

Write It Down: Take a moment to write in a journal about your experience. Write down the qualities or aspects of yourself that you called back. Feel how your body is reacting. Reflect on what you are now ready for—whether it's new opportunities, personal growth, or deeper connections. Acknowledge it again for yourself and say it out loud so your brain hears it.

Here's a summary of the insights and actions to take from the practice to integrate your inner child and nurture your well-being:

1. Legalise and Integrate: Write down the insights gained from your practice. Visualizations, images, and feelings that emerge are valid parts of yourself. Recognise them as integral to who you are and what you can achieve.

2. Thank and Praise Your Inner Child: Show gratitude to your inner child for their strength and resilience. Praise. Tell your inner child, "Well done, my precious. I'm taking you with me now."

3. Daily Engagement: Commit to asking your inner child daily:

What do you want?

Protection, respect, play, fun, attention, love, pleasure, acceptance. Promise to provide these needs yourself.

What can I do for you now?

Regularly check in with your inner child to offer comfort, assurance, and love, cake, chocolate, and toys - give it to yourself. Create a ritual to make your inner child feel safe and cherished within you.

4. Ritual of Care: Establish a ritual to reinforce your inner child's sense of security within you. This could involve visualisation, meditation, affirmations, or physical gestures like hugging yourself.

5. Safe Space: Ensure your inner child feels safe and valued within your heart. Remind yourself that despite external changes, your inner world remains a sanctuary of safety and acceptance.

6. Acceptance and Change: Embrace new thoughts, insights, and energy that emerge from this practice. Allow these changes to unfold naturally in all areas of your life, promoting well-being, health, and inner harmony.

7. Affirmation for Integration: Conclude with the affirmation, "I am giving it time and space. I allow all changes to appear in all areas of my life safely and smoothly for me and for all people around me."

By following these steps, you honour your inner child, nurture your well-being, and cultivate a deeper sense of harmony within yourself. Allow this process to unfold at its own pace, knowing that each step contributes to your healing and growth.

You will notice how more empathetic you will become toward yourself and how your healthy personal boundaries will appear naturally.

Mindfulness Practices

Try to implement a mindful approach to understanding and addressing your emotional responses, fostering greater self-awareness and emotional intelligence.

In an emotional situation, practising mindfulness can help you gain clarity and control over your reactions. Here's a step-by-step guide to mindful reflection in such moments:

1. Pause and Breathe: Take a deep breath. This helps to calm your mind and body, creating a space for reflection rather than reaction.

2. Identify the Reacting Self:

- Ask yourself, "Who inside me is reacting?"
- Recognise the part of you that is triggered. This could be an aspect of your personality, a past experience, or a conditioned response.

3. Acknowledge Vulnerability:

- Ask, "Who inside me feels hurt and vulnerable?"
- Identify the vulnerable part of you. This may be an inner child, a past trauma, or an unmet need.

Whom or what does your inner part see in this person or situation really? What does it remind you of? Or whom it reminds you of?

Why I asked this question is because we project on others our unresolved emotions and unconsciously perceive them incorrectly.

4. Take Responsibility for Hidden Needs:

How can you help yourself?

- Reflect on the needs that are surfacing. What is this part of you longing for? Validation, safety, love, respect? Be perceptive to your inner voice.
- Acknowledge these needs without judgment.

5. Re-evaluate the Situation:

- With a clearer understanding of your inner dynamics, take another breath.
- Consider the situation again, this time from a place of awareness rather than an immediate emotional response.

Body Scan & Release Practice:

1. Scan Your Body

- Find a quiet place and sit or lie down comfortably.
- Close your eyes and take a few deep breaths to centre yourself.
- Slowly scan your body from head to toe, paying attention to any areas of tension, discomfort, or blockage.
- Notice any thoughts, convictions, or memories that arise during this process.

2. Identify & Visualise

- Identify what your body still holds from the past: thoughts, convictions, blockages, or tension, where your body keeps the memory of it
- Visualise these elements clearly in your mind's eye.

3. Release & Validate

- Acknowledge each identified element by saying: "I see you, but I no longer require you."
- Visualise these elements being gently pushed out from your body.

4. Send Them Away

- Mentally send these elements to where they belong, whether it's a situation or a person from your past.
- Say: "I send you where you belong."

5. Reclaim Your True Nature

When you let this tension, thought, and feeling get inside something, yours was pushed away.

- Ask for something that is truly yours to return to you, something that represents your true nature.
- Visualise this positive energy or attribute coming back to you and filling the spaces left by what you released.

6. Accept It

- Accept this positive energy wholeheartedly.
- Feel it filling up your body and mind, restoring you to your true, balanced self.
- Take a few moments to sit with this feeling of wholeness and peace. Write down your insights, and maybe you will choose to direct this energy somewhere good for you.

Practice self-awareness. Use various methods like expressing strong emotions through physical means (e.g., shouting, turning the pillow apart, singing helps too, dancing, sports). Do not let them be stuck in you.

Help yourself with it; all is right as long as it helps you feel better.

After emotional release, ask yourself what parts of your true nature have been pushed away during emotional suppression. Call back these aspects of yourself.

You can do it. It is a matter of practice. You might feel like, in some situations, your self-worth and your self-esteem left you. Call it back from everywhere!

You are self-aware, and you hold control of yourself! Whenever you are overreacting or feel too emotional, check in with your inner child to determine its emotional needs. Ask questions like:

- Who inside me needs my attention now?
- How old is this part of me?
- What scares or offends this part?
- When did these feelings first arise?

- Provide support, reassurance, and safety to your inner child. Remind yourself that you are the only adult who can nurture and protect this vulnerable part of yourself.

Mindful Self-Inquiry:

- Throughout the day, practice mindful self-inquiry. When you notice repetitive thoughts or bodily tension, ask yourself why these thoughts or tensions arise.
- Explore the underlying emotions and experiences behind these patterns. This helps increase self-awareness and understanding of your inner world.

As an example - you understand in a moment that you are emotionally overreacting. You can connect to yourself and ask: What part of me is being triggered now?

Identify your part and acknowledge your feelings; it is all ok. It is part of your psyche; part of your energy wants to be seen and understood.

Look again at the situation and separate two situations and different needs.

If you are overreacting to someone's opinion of you, it is ok. They are not your parents. You are not a child anymore. Let people have their own opinion. Show respect toward their journey, and take a high road.

When someone criticises you, they do the same toward themselves, and it is done to them. All is transparent. Whatever people say about other people, they are basically saying about themselves and contributing to situations where they will be criticised or judged in return.

We are more alike, and we are more connected than we think. And we cannot see in others something that does not exist in us on our world map. You give a compliment - means whatever you compliment is inside you. You say something bad about a person – same fashion – it lives inside you but it is easier to admit when it is someone else.

Habits:

If you want to change patterns of habits, for example, overeating, you need to have a structured approach. Begin by choosing a habit that you want to get rid of, and then follow the steps below to understand and address it:

1. Connect to Your Body: Begin by grounding yourself and tuning into your physical sensations. Take deep breaths and focus on the present moment.

2. Visualize Food: Imagine your favourite foods in front of you. Observe your immediate reactions.

3. Identify Emotions & Feelings: Notice what emotions and physical sensations arise. Are you feeling excited, anxious, comforted, or something else? Collect these emotions and sensations.

4. Explore Subconscious Associations: Ask yourself what your subconscious mind associates with this food. What does it represent to you? Comfort, love, stress relief, or something else?

5. Uncover Deeper Needs: Reflect on whom or what you are trying to connect with through overeating. Is it a need for comfort, security, or perhaps a way to cope with stress?

6. Identify the Inner Self: Determine which part of you is driving this need. Is it a child seeking comfort, an adult dealing with stress, or another aspect of your personality?

7. Find Alternative Solutions: Brainstorm different, healthier ways to meet the underlying needs. This could involve engaging in a hobby, talking to a friend, building connections with immediate family, and relaxation techniques.

By going through this process, you can gain insight into the underlying motivations for your habits and find more effective ways to address them, leading to lasting change.

These practices aim to foster a deeper connection with yourself, promote healing, and cultivate empathy. Embrace them with patience and openness, knowing that each step contributes to your well-being and inner harmony.

Process of deep introspection and self-awareness. Here is your practice:

Exploring Tension & Emotions:

Identify where tension resides in your body. Visualize it on a mental screen and acknowledge its presence.

Ask the tension what it is doing for you and what you need it for. Listen without rationalising or judging.

- Receive the first answer that comes to mind, as it's likely the most genuine response. Find your deepest need and provide for yourself what you need.

Self-Awareness & Acceptance:

Practice unconditional love towards yourself. Accept all feelings and give yourself time and space to experience them fully. Once it is brought to your consciousness, it loses control over you, and you explore ways to heal it.

Understand that there are no mistakes or comparisons in your journey. Your path is unique, and acceptance is the way forward.

Embrace the Process:

- Approach this process as an observer, without judgment or pressure to fix or immediately find solutions.
- Remind yourself that it's a gradual journey of self-discovery and growth. Trust in the process and support yourself truthfully.

Embrace this approach as your new philosophy of life — one centred on self-acceptance, patience, and being present in your own unique experience.

By following these practices, you foster deep self-awareness, acceptance, and unconditional love towards yourself, facilitating inner healing and personal growth. Allow this process to unfold naturally, honouring your own pace and experiences along the way.

Conclusion & Integration:

- Acknowledge that healing and self-awareness are ongoing processes. Embrace the journey of understanding and integrating all parts of yourself.
- Trust in your ability to heal and grow through self-awareness and self-compassion. Seek professional guidance and help if you need it.

Give yourself time! You can use these practices regularly to help release past burdens, stressful situations, and negative interactions and reclaim your natural state of balance and well-being.

Approach Others with Empathy & Respect

When encountering someone who is sad or angry, refrain from judgment. Recognize that their emotions may reflect parts of them that also need attention. Practice empathy and humility. Avoid trying to change people; instead, meet them where they are in their journey and respect their experiences.

Chapter 5:
Our Parents

Without two wings behind you, like Mom and Dad, you will not fly!

Whenever it comes to self-confidence, self-esteem, self-worth, guess what it is all related to? It is our inner connection to our parents, and this is the anchor we need to begin our journey.

The metaphor of being "a tree without roots" powerfully conveys a sense of disconnection, especially from one's lineage or heritage. In many cultures and psychological frameworks, our roots are symbolically tied to our ancestors, particularly our parents, who serve as the primary connection to our past. When someone feels disconnected from their roots, it can indicate a disconnection from their identity, history, or the foundational support system that shaped them.

Restoring that connection often begins with healing the relationship with one's parents, since they are the immediate link to ancestral ties. Even if the relationship with them is complex or strained, working through those emotional and psychological dynamics—whether directly or through internal work—can re-establish a sense of groundedness and continuity.

By reconnecting with your parents and understanding your place in the larger tapestry of family and ancestry, you strengthen your roots, which in turn nourishes your sense of identity and purpose. This can be done through dialogue, therapy, or self-reflection. Understanding our relationship with our parents can save us from endless soul-searching. As children, we unconsciously capture snapshots of our upbringing—a frozen picture that lacks the full truth. We don't see the complete story of why the flow of love may have been disrupted or the personal struggles our parents faced.

Regardless of the nature of our relationship with our parents, they live within us, and their stories shape our own. You can live on the other side of the world, your parents live inside you, and you consist of 100 procents of your mom and <u>100</u> of your father. Rejecting them only distances us from ourselves and amplifies our suffering.

You might notice similarities between your complaints about your partner or friends and the conflicts you had with your parents. These relationships serve as blueprints for how we interact in the world. Unpleasant memories caused by our parents were often unintentional, but clinging to these frozen images perpetuates repeated scenarios and transfers pain further. Everything unresolved with your parents will manifest itself with your partner, colleagues, bosses, etc.

The first reason is that our early familial experiences deeply influence our subconscious understanding of love. We often unconsciously seek out relationships that mirror the dynamics we observed between our parents and our early relationships with our parents, even if we consciously desire something different. This familiarity feels like love to us because it resonates with what we internalized during childhood.

For instance, if your father was emotionally absent, you might find yourself attracted to distant or emotionally unavailable partners. This pattern repeats itself because it is what feels familiar, even if it is not ideal. We may find ourselves in similar relationships repeatedly, complaining about the same issues, until we recognise that these patterns are manifestations of our internalised experiences. Recognising and addressing these unconscious patterns is essential for breaking the cycle and forming healthier relationships.

Whatever qualities we judge and label as bad in our parents, we tend to have exactly the same qualities. If you feel your mom was cold- you might be cold toward yourself - you might be cold toward your kid - you might have chosen a cold partner.

The key is not to judge, and you will not be judged, and you will not repeat what you have been judging! The key lies in getting emotionally separated from our parents as well. Stop projecting on our surroundings our parents. If we do not do that, we will be living in illusions.

By focusing on healing your perception and inner connection with your mother and father, you can transform your broader outlook on life, fostering a greater sense of trust and safety in your everyday experiences.

Also, the key lies in making peace with what we received or didn't receive from our parents. Instead of judging them, we must understand that denying their flaws often leads us to repeat the same patterns. This acceptance allows us to break free from inherited pain and forge healthier relationships moving forward.

There are the psychological dynamics of enmeshed family roles and their long-term impact on adult relationships. Here's how these dynamics manifest in life and affect relationships. This scenario is a form of emotional parentification, where the child steps into the role of the absent partner, often trying to provide emotional support and stability to the remaining parent. This can be especially challenging because the child might feel responsible for the parent's happiness and well-being, which is a heavy burden for them to carry.

Mom's Son / Dad's Daughter Dynamics

Mom's Son (Enmeshed with Mother):

When a son becomes an emotional partner to his mother, he takes on adult responsibilities prematurely, often sacrificing his own needs to keep his mother happy. As an adult, this man may find relationships overwhelming. He might feel that he has to constantly adapt and sacrifice himself to please his partner, echoing his childhood role. The belief that he must make others happy to be valued can lead to a fear of failure in relationships and losing oneself in relationships. Consequently, he might avoid deep connections to evade this perceived burden, leading to a pattern of running from commitment.

Dad's Daughter (Idealises Father)

A daughter who sees her father as the ultimate ideal may set unrealistically high standards for any future partner. No one seems to measure up to the pedestal she has placed her father on. This idealisation can prevent her from forming profound connections with men, as she constantly compares them unfavourably to her father. The constant comparison and unattainable standards can lead to chronic dissatisfaction in relationships, making it difficult for her to find happiness with any partner.

Manifestations in Adult Life

Both types of enmeshment can lead to insecure attachment styles. These individuals might have difficulty trusting others or forming stable, healthy relationships. Their sense of self-worth often becomes dependent on making others happy, leading to codependency. They might neglect their own needs and well-being in relationships. They might either avoid deep relationships to protect themselves from emotional burdens or overcommit and lose their sense of self in the process. Constantly trying to meet the expectations they internalized as children can lead to emotional exhaustion, making it hard to sustain long-term relationships.

Bert Hellinger, the developer of Family Constellations therapy, emphasises the importance of understanding and accepting one's place within the family system. According to his teachings, acknowledging and accepting one's parents and family dynamics is essential for personal success and emotional well-being. Hellinger believes that unresolved family issues and imbalances can hinder an individual's life progress, and through Family Constellations, one can identify and resolve these hidden dynamics to restore harmony and support personal growth.

Developing self-awareness about these patterns and actively working to change them can gradually lead to healthier relationships. This involves recognizing triggers and consciously choosing different responses.

To truly heal and find peace within ourselves, first, we must move beyond superficial respect or hidden judgments toward our parents. It's about genuinely accepting them—everything about them, their lives, choices, personalities, and their relationships, without reservations or inner criticisms. When we accept our parents, we also accept ourselves, embracing the resources inherited from both maternal and paternal generations. By genuinely embracing and agreeing with their relationships as they are or were, we liberate ourselves from unconsciously recreating similar patterns. This conscious acceptance prevents us from trying to rewrite history or prove it could have been different, thereby breaking the cycle of passing down unresolved issues to our children. This deep, sincere acceptance is crucial because it forms the foundation of our self-esteem and self-worth, and it is a base for maturity.

Second, we need to take up our right place, which is a child, no one else for a parent. Rather than unconsciously trying to prove that you can do better or rebelling against your parents, denying any of their patterns or characteristics, you are doomed to repeat it. Even if you try to be the opposite of the trait you disliked, then you might encounter people in your surroundings who will mirror what you deny and judge. At some level, you might see it as unfair punishment, but no, this is the way, as I said, to agree, accept, and finally, love and mature.

Taking your rightful place in the family, the child's role is not a psychological partner and not a parent for your parents, not their judge. When you approach this with sincerity, you'll notice a shift in your energy within the family dynamics. This shift allows you to operate from a place of authenticity and self-awareness. You begin to vibrate differently in this place. You become available for your own life and your relationships. This shift from inner protest to genuine acceptance and gratitude enables you to create your own experiences and navigate relationships from a place of strength and clarity. You're empowered to make choices that align with your true self, not as a reaction to your upbringing or as a means of proving something.

Kindly, regardless of your current relationship with your parents, whether you know them well, haven't seen them in a long time, or never knew them, this practice is about restoring an inner connection with them. Recognise that they are the source of your vitality, connecting you to life itself, and all the strengths and talents of your family lineage flow through them to you. The flow of love emanates from them to you, like a river of life that they initiated by saying yes to your existence. This love flows through you and directs your life towards your goals, desires, and relationships, including those with your spouse and children.

You may have thoughts or feelings about wanting to change things about your parents disagreeing with their choices or relationships. However, acknowledge that they are much older than you, and they did the best they could with what they knew at the time. If they could have done things differently, they would have. As their child, it's important to understand that you cannot change their past decisions; you cannot change anything. Maybe you dreamt about having different parents, or maybe you looked unconsciously for other parents in different people.

The truth is you have parents, and you will not have different parents. No one ever can take up their place. You cannot be born into another family again. If you carry any resentment towards your parents, recognise that this may also reflect a deeper resentment towards yourself and others.

How can you build strong relationships and move forward in your own life if you're unable to accept the fundamental foundation of who you are - your parents. In terms of energy level, you are stuck looking at the past and are not able to direct your energy into the future. Take a few moments to sit with these feelings and insights. Embrace the connection with your parents as an integral part of your identity and acknowledge the love and life they have given you. This will help you to heal and strengthen your inner connection with your parents, fostering a deeper sense of acceptance and gratitude.

Recognise that the gift of life came from your mother and father— no one else in the world has given you anything comparable. Take a moment to reflect on this profound truth. You don't owe them anything in return other than to live your life fully. Your parents gave you life; they do not have to give you anything else.

Direct the energy and love you received from them towards your relationships, children, projects, and ambitious dreams. Your mother is the greatest woman, and your father is the greatest man. They are a perfect match; your mother is the best woman for your father, and your father is the best man for your mother. Even if they are not together now, in your heart, they will always be united as the couple who brought you into this world. You agree with their relationships. Your place is the place of the child. The stream of life energy flowing from both your mother and father to you and these energies blending within you. You are made up of both your mother's and father's energies. Allow yourself to feel how their energies mix and intermingle inside you. You do not have to choose between your mother or your father—both are a part of you. In some ways, you are like your mother, and in other ways, you are like your father. Feel the wholeness and completeness inside yourself. You are a beautiful amalgamation of your parents' love and life energies. Embrace all aspects of yourself. You do not need to suppress any part of who you are or try to change yourself. You are enough just as you are. You are a living miracle that embodies the love between your parents— a testament to their union and love for each other.

Feel the solidity and strength of the foundation within your body, built from the energies of your mother and father. You know who you are, and you know that you are loved and supported. Accept what they can give you without demanding more. You have to connect with their unconditional love and support, feeling their souls always by your side, supporting you in every moment.

Take a moment to sit with this feeling of unity and connectedness with your roots. Allow yourself to be embraced by the love that flows from your parents to you, grounding you in your identity and strength. No one else can do that for you, and this connection runs in your blood. By healing it, you heal yourself.

Take a few moments to absorb these feelings and insights that arise while you are reading. This practice helps to heal and strengthen your inner connection with your parents, fostering a deeper sense of acceptance, gratitude, self-love and self-acceptance.

If you can do that, please kneel in front of your parents, either physically, if possible or in your imagination if they are no longer with you. Feel the humility and reverence in this act as you seek their blessings.

Whether in reality or in the imagination, understand that your parents are always with you. Your brain does not distinguish between reality and imagination; the same neural pathways are activated. Embrace this connection.

The most crucial aspect of this is your attitude. Embrace and accept your parents' lives exactly as they are. Respect their paths and decisions, and cultivate a deep sense of gratitude for the life they have given you. You cannot take up any other role, only yours - their child.

Through this unconditional love and acceptance, you will be able to stop repeating the same scenarios, forsake your life, try to fix it, and start directing your energy toward your life.

While reading, you can visualise yourself standing with your parents behind you, supporting you as you face forward on your life's journey. Feel the strength and grounding that comes from this connection.

Take a moment to feel your body and welcome any sensations that arise during this practice. Allow yourself to absorb the feelings of acceptance, gratitude, and connection with your roots.

Reflect on your insights and experiences. Write down any realisations or feelings that came up during this process. This reflection helps solidify the healing and strengthening of your inner connection with your parents.

Your inner connection to acceptance, respect, and gratitude is the most important. Your relationships with your parents in the physical world might vary, but your inner connection will foster a deeper sense of peace, acceptance, and love for them, ultimately contributing to your own well-being and self-awareness.

Bear in mind that your right place in the family system is the place of a child; no one else's roles can be carried out by you. This place gives

The Flow of Energy in Parent-Child Relationships. In the dynamic between parents and children, the flow of energy and support is unidirectional:

There is solid 100% truth in the system that:

1. Parents Give Life:

Parents provide the gift of life, nurturing, and resources to their children. This flow of energy from parent to child is natural and foundational.

2. Children Accept & Pass On:

As children grow, they accept this energy and the responsibilities it entails. Their role is to pass this energy forward, either to their own children or to the world around them, through their actions and contributions.

What happens when we judge, deny, reject, disrespect or parent our parents – a disruption of natural flow occurs. When children attempt to give energy back to their parents, it disrupts this natural flow. Questions like why I do not have energy for my family, kids, work, etc.

This is why:

By directing energy upward to their parents, children inadvertently close the energetic system. This disrupts the balance and depletes the resources necessary for the system to thrive.

Lack of Continuity

The closed system lacks the necessary resource flow to continue effectively. The natural progression of life energy, support, and nurturing is hindered, affecting both generations.

Maintaining Balance

1. Accepting the Gift:

Children should accept the life and resources provided by their parents with gratitude, using them to grow, develop, and eventually pass on to the next generation.

2. Passing Forward:

The focus should be on forwarding the energy and support received, ensuring a continuous, healthy flow within the family and the broader community.

3. Supporting, Not Parenting, Parents:

While it's important to care for ageing parents, this should be done without disrupting the natural flow. Emotional and physical support should be balanced with maintaining one's own life energy and passing it forward.

Everything remains the same in the physical world; however, you extended your view on your parents to get connected to the vital energy flow for your own life.

Magic happens when you agree, accept and feel gratitude.

Understanding and respecting this natural flow ensures that the energy within families and generations remains vital and productive. It encourages a healthy cycle of giving, receiving, and passing forward, creating a sustainable system of support and growth.

Decide what you can do in the physical world to reconnect with your parents - have a sincere conversation, maybe send flowers to your mom or give a gift to your father. Gratitude and fewer complaints, resentment, etc., and ask them for their blessings with whatever you wish.

I recommend this practice of forgiveness because it is deep and transformative. It will literally release lots of energy and heal the inner conflicts.

Emotions—whether positive or negative—can create long-lasting energetic connections between people, even across great physical distances. When individuals hold onto negative emotions like resentment, anger, or unresolved conflict, it can sustain a form of attachment that persists on an energetic level. This connection may influence their thoughts, moods, and behaviors, even if they are no longer in contact physically.

In psychology and energy work, it's believed that such unresolved emotions can create energetic cords or ties that bind people together. These connections, especially when rooted in negative emotions, can drain emotional energy and keep both parties stuck in the past. Releasing or resolving these feelings is often essential for breaking the energetic link and restoring balance in one's life. This could involve forgiveness, acceptance, or deeper self-reflection to free oneself from the emotional weight.

Prepare for the Practice:

Choose a person with whom you need to practice forgiveness. It could be your mom, your father, your ex-partner, your friend, or anyone significant in your life who you feel changed you in a way that is still very much alive in you and emotionally charged.

I will put it this way. You can also practice this with anyone you want to balance your emotional reaction and get it to neutral or, better, to a state of gratitude.

Get a piece of paper and a pen to write down your feelings and thoughts without any corrections.

1. Express Your Truth:

Imagine the person in front of you or visualise them clearly in your mind's eye. Begin by stating, "I want to tell you…" and write down everything that has hurt or offended you. Be completely honest and raw when expressing your feelings.

Continue with, "I want to tell you about something that was never talked about and was scary to even think about." Write down any suppressed emotions or experiences.

Go deeper: "I want to tell you what was forgotten, and I didn't want to admit…" Write down any buried feelings or memories.

- Express the most unpleasant feelings: "I want to tell you about my anger, rage, powerlessness, hopelessness…" Write down all your emotions without filtering.

2. Empathise with Their Perspective:

Now, imagine yourself stepping into their shoes. Feel as if you are them, experiencing their emotions and thoughts. Allow your psyche to reveal their version of events. Listen to their perspective, their fears, hurts, and true intentions. Trust the answers that come from within you. Understand that hurtful actions often stem from inner pain and neglect.

3. Return to Yourself:

After empathising with their perspective, return to your own body. Take note of how you feel now that you have a fuller understanding.

4. Practice Forgiveness:

Say aloud or write down, "I forgive you for…" and list specific grievances. Release the emotional weight associated with each item. If there's something you can't forgive yet, acknowledge it: "I can't forgive you for this yet, but I'm willing to work towards forgiveness." Express anything else you need to say: "I want to tell you…" and speak your truth.

5. Ask for Forgiveness:

Reflect on your own actions and ask for forgiveness from the person: "Forgive me for…" Describe what you're seeking forgiveness for, and forgive yourself as well.

6. Express Gratitude:

Finally, express gratitude: "I thank you for…" and describe what you're thankful for. Repeat this step for each significant realisation or aspect of the practice.

7. Acknowledge Your Journey:

Recognise the depth of what you've done. It's okay to feel emotional; crying can be a natural release after such a profound practice. Trust that these actions will bring about positive changes in yourself and your relationships.

This practice aims to heal wounds, foster empathy, and cultivate forgiveness within yourself and towards others. It's a powerful tool for emotional healing and growth.

Chapter 6:
Relationships

The strongest human hunger is a hunger for genuine love.

Like in the song by the Beatles, "All you need is love". However, often, blind love prevents us from truly experiencing love.

We enter relationships hoping not to get hurt. However, it is impossible to build genuine, deep connections without being open and honest. Another person will hurt you just like you will hurt back; it is inevitable. Only through this way can the connection grow into a beautiful relationship.

I will give you a metaphor.

When you think about a Union, partnership or marriage.

Imagine a bag with two stones with sharp edges, and the more they rub against each other, the smoother they become. The task is not to tear the bag out but to preserve it and make it smooth.

All relationships should begin with self-reflection and self-awareness. We cannot change others; therefore, understanding how people and situations reflect aspects of ourselves is crucial. Embracing relationships as opportunities for self-learning fosters personal growth and deeper connections with others.

It's essential to revisit the connection between our emotional state and our relationships, especially concerning our parents. Remaining emotionally attached to our parents can keep us in a perpetual state of childhood regardless of our actual age. This emotional attachment can lead us to unconsciously project our unmet needs for parental love onto our partners. It's crucial to realize that no partner can fully replace or fulfil these parental needs, and this projection can significantly impact our sexual lives and overall satisfaction in relationships. Whatever he or she does will never be enough.

Your inner space for your partner is formed long before you meet one. This inner space holds your beliefs, conscious and unconscious. The partner comes and, as if starting to lighten up those areas. The light appears where there is darkness.

Relationships serve as profound mirrors for self-discovery and growth. To deepen our understanding of ourselves within relationships, it's beneficial to reflect on several key questions:

Motivation for Relationships:

What kind of need initially motivated me to enter into this relationship? It's crucial to answer honestly to uncover underlying motivations.

1. Purpose of Relationships:

What does this relationship mean to me? Define its significance and purpose in your life.

2. Personal Happiness:

Was I content with my life before entering this partnership? Reflect on your personal happiness and fulfilment independently of your relationship.

3. Needs and Fulfillment:

What needs am I seeking to fulfil through this relationship? Identify your emotional, psychological, and physical needs.

4. Emotional Connection:

Do I experience joy and acceptance when I am with this person? Evaluate the emotional quality of the connection.

5. Communication:

Are difficult conversations openly communicated or avoided? Assess the communication dynamics within the relationship.

6. Desired Relationship Dynamics:

What do I envision for our relationship? Define your ideal relationship dynamics and compare them with the current reality.

7. Personal Contribution:

What am I actively doing to make this relationship work? Evaluate your efforts and contributions.

8. Communication of Needs:

Do I effectively communicate my desires and expectations, or do I expect my partner to guess them?

9.Mutual Contribution:

Does my partner contribute equally to the relationship, or does the burden fall disproportionately on me?

10. Reciprocity:

Do I feel balanced in giving and receiving within this relationship? Assess the reciprocity of emotional and practical support.

11. Awareness of Partner's Needs:

How often do I inquire about my partner's unmet needs and actively work to fulfil them?

12. Love Languages:

Am I aware of my own love language? Do I understand my partner's love language? Understanding these can enhance communication and intimacy.

To rekindle love and prevent taking each other for granted, consider asking:

Expressions of Love: How do you know that I love you? Explore specific actions and behaviours that communicate love effectively.

Mutual Happiness: What actions or gestures make you feel happiest in our relationship?

Memorable Moments: What memories of us do you cherish?

When it comes to building relationships, the concept of balance between give and take is fundamental to all relationships. Whether in personal or professional settings, this balance ensures harmony, respect, and mutual growth. When one person gives too much, and the other cannot or will not reciprocate, an energetic imbalance occurs. One is left waiting to receive back, and another is running and maybe even devaluing another, not being able to reciprocate back.

This often leads to unresolved tension, unspoken expectations, and deep frustration, creating a cycle that can last even beyond physical separation.

It forms energetic ties that are especially profound. When one person feels overburdened by giving, they may develop resentment, while the other feels overwhelmed by the pressure to reciprocate, often leading them to withdraw. These energetic bonds can persist, trapping both people in a state of emotional unrest, even if they are no longer together physically.

In conflict, the escalation of negative exchanges—where one tries to return harm with even greater harm—fuels a cycle of destruction. It perpetuates the war between individuals, whether in a divorce, workplace conflict, or any strained relationship. This is how negative bonds are maintained, even though people believe they are trying to break free.

The Law of Balance, when followed consciously, can transform relationships. Instead of fueling resentment or competition over who gives more or receives less, it can cultivate love, respect, and mutual appreciation. Small acts of giving, met with slightly greater acts of kindness in return, create a positive feedback loop. This builds not only love in personal relationships but also trust and collaboration in professional ones.

In all aspects of life, recognising and honouring this balance can lead to healthier connections and lasting peace. It requires awareness, humility, and a willingness to give and receive in a way that nurtures both parties, respecting each person's capacity and contribution.

Guided Inner Work:

It's insightful to reflect on the dynamics of your relationship through self-awareness and introspection. This exercise encourages you to connect with your emotions, recognize the underlying causes of your feelings, and understand how past experiences might influence your current interactions.

By imagining your partner next to you and observing your emotions, you can start identifying the specific triggers that cause distress. Ask yourself:

1. What emotions do I feel toward my partner right now?

2. What do I want to say or do in response to these emotions?

3. Who within me is suffering or feels hurt? It is part of you; not all of you are unhappy with your partner. See this part of you.

4. Whom do I really see in my partner—my current partner or someone from my past? Ask yourself and listen to an inner answer; your psyche will collaborate. Make sure you are in a peaceful place where no one can interfere.

5. What does my partner's behaviour remind me of?

6. What do I need right now to feel understood and supported?

Acknowledging these feelings can help you understand whether you're projecting unresolved emotions from past relationships, such as those with your parents, onto your partner. This unconscious projection can lead to unrealistic expectations and misunderstandings.

Once you recognise this, communicate openly with your partner. Express your feelings and needs clearly, and take responsibility for the emotions that are yours to manage. This can alleviate the emotional burden on both of you, fostering a more understanding and supportive relationship.

Next, it is paramount that all our relationships are finished properly. Each subsequent partner is responsible for the previous one. We recreate the same scenario. Any connection that is not closed emotionally consumes a lot of energy; the more open unfinished relationships, the less energy we have.

Guided inner work focused on reclaiming energy from past emotional attachments and fostering self-awareness and growth. Here's a structured approach to guide you through this process:

Guided Inner Work Practice

Find Your Safe Place:

Visualise a serene, safe place where you feel calm and comfortable. It could be a beach, a forest, a cosy room—anywhere you feel at peace.

1. Relax and Let Go:

Take deep breaths and relax your body and mind. Let go of all thoughts and distractions. Feel the peace and calm of your chosen place.

2. Invite the Person:

Imagine the person with whom you have an emotional attachment standing before you in your safe place.

3. Switch to Inner Observer Mode:

Shift into an observer mindset. Notice your feelings, grievances, expectations, dreams, and desires related to this person. Write them down without judgment.

You can even ask your subconscious whom you see in your partner.

4. Retrieve Your Energy:

Visualise all the energy you've invested in this emotional attachment as a large balloon. State aloud, "Now I need my energy back. I am reclaiming it now." Feel the warmth as your energy returns to your body, revitalising your mind, body, and spirit.

5.Explore Emotions & Beliefs:

Reflect on the emotions that keep you attached and the beliefs that sustain this connection. Ask yourself what part of you is still holding on. Write down any insights that arise.

6. Identify Unmet Needs:

Ask your inner self what you are still waiting for or needing from this person. Listen to the answer attentively. Write down the needs and desires that surface. (feel now if maybe you mistaken him or her with your mom or your father)

Meet Your Needs Differently:

Brainstorm ways to meet these needs in healthier, self-supportive ways. Write down actionable steps you can take to fulfil these needs independently.

7. Release Expectations:

Look at the person without your expectations. Express gratitude for the experience gained. Consider their expectations of you with respect; however, return them and acknowledge both the positive and negative aspects of your interactions.

8.Recognise Intention and Experience:

Acknowledge that neither of you had bad intentions. Recognize that actions stemmed from a need to be heard, loved, and understood. Accept the experiences exchanged as part of growth.

9. Commit to Self-Care and Change:

Write down what you want for yourself moving forward. You will take detailed actions daily, weekly, and monthly to nurture yourself and promote well-being. The list of changes you are ready for in your relationships and friendships.

10. Closing Affirmation:

Affirm your commitment to self-awareness and growth. Say aloud, "I am finishing this connection within me. I am giving time and space for the changes I need for my well-being. I will take from this practice exactly what I need."

11. Self-Nourishment:

End by embracing yourself with self-love and self-compassion. Reward yourself with anything that brings you joy or comfort.

Relationships are indeed complex interactions where our expectations often clash with the reality of others' needs and desires. Here's a reflection on nurturing healthier relationships:

Reflection on Relationships

Mutual Needs & Expectations:

Recognise that relationships involve not just you and your partner but also your mutual expectations. Understand that both parties have needs and desires that deserve acknowledgement and respect.

1. Humanizing Others:

Shift your perspective to see the humanity in others. Instead of viewing them solely through the lens of what they can provide for you, consider their own desires and aspirations.

2. Embracing Growth Through Communication:

Genuine growth in relationships starts with open communication and closeness. Embrace maturity by fostering honest, respectful dialogue about needs, boundaries, and aspirations.

3. Honesty and Closure:

Be courageous enough to acknowledge when a relationship lacks vitality or no longer serves both parties. Approach conversations about potential closure with honesty, respect, and gratitude for the experiences shared.

4.Avoiding Abrupt Endings:

Abruptly cutting off relationships out of anger or frustration can lead to repeated patterns or unforeseen emotional upheavals in the future. Practice closure with clarity and compassion.

5. Fairness and Reciprocity:

Trust in the inherent fairness of life where reciprocity plays a significant role. What you give in relationships often mirrors what you receive, highlighting the importance of authenticity and reciprocity.

Conclusion

By embracing these reflections, you can cultivate relationships grounded in mutual understanding, respect, and growth. Remember, every interaction is an opportunity for personal and relational development, fostering connections that honour both your needs and those of others.

Also I would like to share with you in this chapter another piece of wisdom – "The Prayer" by Fritz Perls, with sound and additions by Jorge Bucay.

I am me; you are you.

I did not come into this world to live up to your expectations, and I know you did not come into this world to live up to mine.

Because I am me, you are you.

When we meet, it will be wonderful.

And if, having met, we do not meet, well, nothing can be done.

Thank you!

Thank you, and goodbye...... I am responsible for moving away from what hurts me.

I am responsible for protecting myself from those who harm me.

I am responsible for paying attention to what is happening to me and assessing my share of participation in what is happening.

I must realize the resonance that my action has. In order for what is happening to happen to me, I must do what I do.

I am not saying that I can control everything that happens to me - no, but I am responsible for everything that happens to me because, in some small way, I contributed to it.

I cannot control the opinions of everyone around me, but I can control mine. I can freely dispose of my actions.

I must decide how I will act. With my limitations, with my troubles, with my ignorance, with all that I have learned and know.

Taking all this into account, I must decide how to act in this way. And I must act in this way.

I must know myself better so that I know my resources.

I must love myself enough to share my privileges and know that this is my decision.

Then, I will have what comes with autonomy, which is the reverse of giving up freedom: courage.

I will have the courage to act as I dictate to my conscience and to pay for it.

Then I will be free, even if the other person doesn't like it.

And if you don't love me the way I am,

And if you poke me the way I am,

And if on the longest and coldest winter night… you leave me alone and go away… Close the door, do you hear? Because there's a draft with me.

Close the door. If this is your decision, close the door.

I won't ask you to stay even a minute against your will. I ask you: close the door, because I live here, and it's cold outside.

And this will be my decision.

This turns me into a person and not a variable manipulator.

Because a self-dependent person cannot be manipulated, and we know that no one can control him.

Because a self-dependent person can be controlled if only he himself wants it, since he is uncontrollable, you do not control him. He is the one who controls the repair; he controls himself.

This means a huge step forward in your personal history and in your development; it implies a completely different way of life and, perhaps, a deeper knowledge of other people.

If you are truly independent, if you do not allow them to manipulate even the smallest thing, then there is a possibility that some people will leave your life… Maybe someone will not dare.

Well, the same thing, influence and at this price.

The price will consist of parting with small particles from our close circle.

And I am preparing to celebrate the appearance of new faces (possibly…).

When we make a decision to do something with another person - something like sex, or less necessary, like a walk in the square (and maybe as necessary as a walk in the square, and as insignificant as sex), we must realize that this is a voluntary decision, thought out as a joint action with another person, but not "for" him, but "with" him. It is important to begin to realize that our relationship with the world, with those around us, and with those close to us in the process consists of actions "with" them.

And that this decision is autonomous and depends on our free choice.

That I do nothing for the sake of another, and therefore he owes me nothing.

That he does nothing for me, and therefore I owe him nothing.

That we just do some things together.

I am happy about it.

In this case, I will not become dependent on him and will not try to make him dependent on me.

I will not damage his dignity by trying to make him afraid.

I will refuse the device that made him hate me.

I will reject sacrifices so that he will never feel sorry for me.

I will not try to become indispensable to him.

I will be content with his love or dislike.

Anyway, if he does not love me, let him not worry about me; there will always be someone who is capable of loving me.

Chapter 7:
Your Goals

Understanding Your Goals

You've done a tremendous amount of work on yourself. Now, it's time to explore your goals. In this chapter, I will outline practical tools to help you work toward your goals. These methods can be applied whenever you find yourself procrastinating, feeling fearful or anxious, and recognising that the root cause may be more psychological than anything else.

Approach this process with patience and mindfulness, giving yourself as much time as you need between each practice. Start with these foundational questions:

1. Why do you want to achieve this goal?

2. What do you hope will happen as a result?

3. How will achieving this goal change the way you feel?

4. How will it change your relationships with people?

Take your time to write down your answers and reflect on them. This initial step is crucial in understanding the deeper motivations behind your goals.

Practice 1: Clarifying Your Goal

Step 1: Define Your Goal

Write down your goal in clear, specific terms. Make sure it is measurable and attainable.

Step 2: Visualise the Outcome

Close your eyes and visualise achieving your goal. See yourself in that moment, experiencing success. Notice the details of your surroundings, your feelings, and the reactions of those around you.

Step 3: Feel the Emotions

Pay attention to the emotions that arise during your visualization. Are you feeling joy, relief, excitement, or something else? Write these emotions down.

Practice 2: Breaking Down Your Goal

Step 1: Identify Milestones

Break your goal into smaller, manageable milestones. What are the key steps you need to take to achieve your goal?

Step 2: Create an Action Plan

For each milestone, write down the actions you need to take. Be specific about what, when, and how you will accomplish each step.

Step 3: Set Deadlines

Assign deadlines to each milestone. Make sure these deadlines are realistic and achievable.

Practice 3: Addressing Obstacles

Step 1: Identify Potential Obstacles

Think about the challenges you might face in achieving your goal. Write down any obstacles you can foresee.

Step 2: Develop Strategies

For each obstacle, develop a strategy to overcome it. Consider resources and support systems.

Practice 4: Identifying Emotions That Stop You

Step-by-Step Guide:

Set Up Your Goal

Take an A4 sheet of paper and write down your goal. Place this sheet in front of you.

1. Create Space for Movement

Make sure you have enough space to take several steps forward.

2. First Step Toward the Goal

Take a step toward the goal. Pause and notice what emotions and feelings arise. Write these down.

3. Second Step Toward the Goal

Take another step closer to your goal. Again, pause and notice any new emotions or feelings. Write these down.

4. Third Step Toward the Goal

Continue stepping closer to your goal, pausing each time to notice and record your emotions and physical sensations.

5. Identify Emotions and Feelings

Examples of emotions might include anxiety, fear, excitement, or uncertainty. Pay attention to both emotional and physical responses (e.g., tension in your shoulders, a knot in your stomach).

6. Separate Your Feelings from Your Goal

Take a second A4 sheet of paper and write down all the feelings and emotions you identified. Your goal remains on the first sheet.

7. Acknowledge the Difference

Remind yourself: "My goal is only a goal." Understand that the goal itself is not inherently scary; it's your past experiences and emotions that are influencing your perception.

8. Recognise Misplaced Feelings

Write down, without correcting, what you realize you have mistaken for your goal (e.g., fear of failure, past disappointments).

9.Admit and Accept Your Feelings

Acknowledge your feelings and experiences out loud: "I admit and accept all my feelings and my experience, and I give them time and space. I see that I have mistaken these feelings for my goal, and I now separate my previous experiences from my goal."

10. Identify the Inner Part

Ask yourself who inside you feels these emotions. What does this part of you need in order not to feel overwhelmed or afraid? Write down the answers you receive.

11. Support Your Inner Needs

Acknowledge these needs and think of practical ways to support yourself. Write down what you will do to address these misleading feelings and take care of them.

Example:

Goal: Start my own business

Emotions Identified: Anxiety, fear of failure, excitement

Physical Sensations: Tightness in chest, butterflies in stomach

Separate Feelings:

Goal Sheet: Start my own business

Feelings Sheet: Anxiety, fear of failure, excitement, tightness in the chest, butterflies in the stomach.

Realisations:

"My goal is only a goal. I have mistaken my goal with past failures and fear of not being good enough."

Acknowledgement:

"I admit and accept all my feelings and my experience, and I give them time and space. I see that I have mistaken these feelings for my goal, and I now separate my previous experiences from my goal."

Inner Needs:

"The part of me that feels anxious needs reassurance and a clear plan."

"I will support myself by setting small, achievable milestones and seeking mentorship."

Actions:

Create a detailed business plan with milestones.

- Find a mentor or join a support group for aspiring entrepreneurs.
- Practice daily affirmations to build confidence.

By following this practice, you can clarify your emotions, separate them from your goals, and create a supportive plan to achieve your aspirations without being held back by past experiences.

Exploring Secondary Benefits: Practices to Uncover Hidden Motivations

Practice 5: Worst-Case Scenario

What's the Worst Thing That Will Happen if You Start Moving Toward Your Goal?

Write down all possible negative outcomes that you fear might happen if you start pursuing your goal. Reflect on these fears and consider how realistic they are and what steps you can take to mitigate them.

Practice 6: Potential Gains and Losses

What Will You Gain if You Achieve Your Goal?

List all the positive outcomes and benefits you will experience if you successfully achieve your goal.

1.What Will You Lose if You Achieve Your Goal?

Identify any potential negative consequences or sacrifices you might need to make to achieve your goal. Reflect on these losses to understand if they are creating resistance toward achieving your goal.

Practice 7: Benefits of Inaction

What Will You Gain/Keep/Have if You Do Not Pursue Your Goal at All?

List the benefits of maintaining your current situation and not pursuing your goal. These benefits often reveal the secondary gains that keep you from taking action.

1. What Will You Lose if You Do Not Pursue Your Goal?

Consider the opportunities and experiences you will miss out on if you choose not to pursue your goal.

Example Reflection

Goal: Start my own business

Practice 1: Worst-Case Scenario:

Practice 2: Potential Gains and Losses

- Fear of financial loss
- Fear of failure and embarrassment
- Fear of losing current job security

What Will You Gain if You Achieve Your Goal?

What Will You Lose if You Achieve Your Goal?

- Financial independence
- Personal fulfilment
- Opportunity to be my own boss
- Job security
- Time with family and friends
- Predictable income

Practice 3: Benefits of Inaction

What Will You Gain/Keep/Have if You Do Not Pursue Your Goal at All?

- Job security and steady income
- Less stress and risk
- More time for current hobbies and family

What Will You Lose if You Do Not Pursue Your Goal?

- Opportunity for personal growth
- Potential financial independence
- Sense of achievement and fulfillment

Reflection

After completing these practices, take some time to reflect on your answers.

Identify Patterns:

Look for recurring themes in your fears and secondary benefits.

1. Evaluate Realism:

Assess how realistic your fears and secondary benefits are.

2. Plan Action Steps:

Develop a plan to address your fears and mitigate potential losses.

Identify ways to minimize the impact of sacrifices you need to make.

Conclusion

By exploring these practices, you can uncover the hidden motivations and secondary benefits that may be holding you back. Understanding these factors allows you to address them consciously, enabling you to move forward more confidently toward your goals. Take your time with each practice, and revisit your reflections periodically to gain deeper insights and adjust your approach as needed.

Practise 8: The "Why" Uncovering Your True Motivation

Instructions:

Identify Your Goal:

Clearly define the goal you are aiming to achieve.

1. Ask "Why" Repeatedly:

Ask yourself why you want to achieve this goal.

Answer the question honestly.

For each answer, ask "why" again.

Repeat this process at least 10 times or until you reach a deep, genuine need or motivation.

Example Exercise:

Goal: Start my own business

Why do I want to start my own business?

Because I want to be my own boss.

1.Why do I want to be my own boss?

Because I want more control over my work.

2.Why do I want more control over my work?

Because I want to create a flexible schedule.

3.Why do I want a flexible schedule?

Because I want to spend more time with my family.

4.Why do I want to spend more time with my family?

Because I feel like I am missing out on important moments.

5. Why do I feel like I am missing out on important moments?

Because my current job demands long hours.

6. Why does my current job demand long hours?

Because the workload is high, and I have little autonomy.

7. Why do I have little autonomy at work?

Because I am not in a leadership position.

8. Why do I want to be in a leadership position?

Because I believe I can make better decisions for my well-being.

9.Why do I believe I can make better decisions for my well-being?

Because I want to feel more fulfilled and balanced in life.

Reflection:

Identify Core Motivation:

Through this exercise, it becomes clear that the true motivation behind starting a business is to feel more fulfilled and balanced in life, particularly through spending more time with family and having greater autonomy.

1. Evaluate Genuine Need:

The genuine need uncovered might be love and connection with family, along with personal fulfilment.

2. Decide if You Still Want It:

Reflect on whether achieving this goal is the best way to meet your true needs. Consider other ways to fulfil this need, such as finding a job with a better work-life balance or creating more family time in your current schedule.

Conclusion:

Understanding the true motivation behind your goals helps you align your actions with your deepest needs. It also allows you to evaluate whether pursuing the goal is the most effective way to meet those needs or if there are alternative paths to fulfilment. The love and acceptance you seek can often be provided by yourself, enhancing your self-worth and inner peace.

Guided Practice 9: Retrieving Stuck Energy from the Past

Instructions:

Find a Quiet Space:

Choose a comfortable and safe place where you can focus without interruptions.

1. Relax and Center Yourself:

Take a few deep breaths.

Relax your head, forehead, and eyes.

Feel your body and let go of all thoughts and inner dialogues.

2. Visualise a Big Screen:

Imagine a large screen in front of you.

This screen will display the situation or person where your energy is stuck.

3. Ask Your Psyche for Guidance:

Ask yourself, "What kind of experience from my past holds most of my energy?"

Allow the situation or person to appear on the screen.

4. Identify the Connection:

Observe what keeps you connected to this situation or person.

Ask, "Who inside me is connected to this?"

Identify the need that was tied to this experience. Listen to your heart and turn off your rational thoughts.

5. Acknowledge Your Need:

Admit to yourself, "Yes, I wanted that, but even if it is painful, I have to admit I will not get what I want here."

6. Visualise the Energy:

See how much of your energy is tied up in this situation.

Imagine a separate image of all the desires, dreams, and expectations you have invested.

7. Reclaim Your Energy:

Say aloud, "Right now, I take everything that belongs to me with me and return with respect to what belongs to this situation."

Visualise yourself taking back all your energy.

Feel the energy returning to your body, mind, and spirit.

8. Close the Situation:

Declare, "Right now, I am finishing the situation within myself. I close it on all levels—my consciousness, my energy, my psyche—in order to move forward."

Visualise the situation becoming smaller, lifeless, and eventually turning into a small black-and-white dot on the screen.

9.Reflect and Redirect Your Energy:

Notice how your body feels now.

Pay attention to the thoughts crossing your mind and where they compel you to direct your renewed energy.

10. Repeat as Needed:

Repeat this practice until you feel that all your energy is reclaimed and the situation no longer triggers a reaction inside you.

Reflection:

> Feel Your Body: Notice any changes in how your body feels after reclaiming your energy.

- **Direct Your Energy:** Think about where you can now direct this reclaimed energy—towards your goals, relationships, or personal growth.
- **Journal:** Write down any thoughts, feelings, or insights that come up during this practice. This will help you understand your inner processes better and keep track of your progress.

By retrieving your energy from past experiences, you free up valuable resources to focus on your present goals and future aspirations. This practice can be repeated as often as necessary to ensure you have all the energy you need to move forward effectively.

Practice 10: Understanding & Integrating Conflicting Parts

Instructions:

Find a Quiet and Comfortable Space:

Ensure you are in a safe and serene environment where you can focus without interruptions.

1. Relax and Center Yourself:

Take a few deep breaths.

Let go of all thoughts and inner dialogues.

Feel your body and become present in the moment.

2. Identify the Part That Wants:

Focus on the part of you that desires to achieve your goal.

Ask this part, "What do you want? What can I do for you?"

Salute this part, give her space, and acknowledge her needs.

3. Invite the Part That Doesn't Want:

Now, focus on the part that is resisting or reluctant to move towards the goal.

Ask this part, "What is she or he protecting me from?"

Listen carefully to understand her concerns and needs.

4. Dialogue Between Parts:

Imagine both parts standing before you.

Introduce them to one another and acknowledge both their perspectives.

Say aloud, "I see you both. You are both important to me. I am giving you each a place."

5. Acknowledge Both Needs:

From your adult self, observe and understand the needs of both parts.

Express appreciation for each part's role in your well-being and harmony.

Acknowledge that both parts are essential for your overall balance and growth.

6. Facilitate a Conversation:

Facilitate a dialogue between the two parts.

Encourage them to share their perspectives with each other.

Ensure they both feel heard and respected.

7. Create a Plan for Integration:

Ask both parts how they can work together to support your goal.

Formulate a plan that honours both their needs and allows for mutual cooperation.

Write down any agreements or understandings reached during this conversation.

8. Reflect on the Process:

Reflect on how you feel after this practice.

Notice any changes in your mindset or emotions regarding your goal.

Write down any insights or realizations that emerged during the dialogue.

Reflection:

Feel Your Body: Notice how your body feels after integrating these parts. Is there a sense of relief, peace, or understanding?

- **Direct Your Energy:** Think about how you can now move forward with both parts working harmoniously towards your goal.
- **Journal:** Document your experience, any shifts in perspective, and any new commitments or actions you plan to take.

By understanding and integrating conflicting parts within yourself, you create a balanced and supportive inner environment that allows you to move forward with clarity and purpose. This practice can be repeated whenever you encounter inner resistance or conflicting desires. When one part of you is dead tired, and another one wants to create a project. You first rest and then go forward with the project.

Practice 11: Reference Point Therapy Practice

Instructions:

Prepare & Calm Yourself:

Find a quiet and comfortable space where you won't be disturbed.

Sit down in a comfortable position.

Close your eyes and take several deep breaths. Inhale deeply, hold for a moment, and then exhale slowly.

Relax your face, forehead, shoulders, spine, arms, and legs.

1. Recall a Situation:

Bring to mind a specific situation where you did something you are not proud of. This could be a time when you wanted to act one way but ended up acting differently due to overwhelming emotions.

Hold this situation in your mind.

2. Connect to Your Body:

Place your hand on your head.

Listen to the thoughts and beliefs you had during that situation. What were you telling yourself? What did you believe at that moment?

Write down these thoughts and beliefs without any corrections or judgments.

3. Acknowledge Your Emotions:

Move your hand to your heart.

Bring up the emotions that these thoughts evoked. Allow yourself to feel and acknowledge all your feelings.

Write down these emotions honestly, without filtering.

4. Recognise Your Bodily Reactions:

Place your hand on your lower belly.

Tune into what your body wanted to do in that situation. Did you want to run, fight, freeze, fawn, disappear, shout, become small, avoid confrontation, hide, etc.?

Feel these impulses and write them down.

5. Support Yourself and Create a New Reality:

Hold your hand on your lower belly and speak to yourself:

"Now I see it. I accept and admit my instinct to [name the instinct, e.g., run] and how it supports my safety."

"I admit all my thoughts, feelings, and emotions. And right now, I admit that I do not have to [name the instinct] to feel safe! I choose my reality, where I can stay and do what I want to do. I choose the appropriate right action, and it will be safe for me!"

Repeat these affirmations, ensuring they resonate deeply within you.

6.   Reclaim Your Energy:

Visualise the energy you spent on this strategy as a big cloud of light.

Imagine reclaiming this energy for a new strategy and new decisions.

Let this energy fill your body, starting from your head and moving down to your shoulders, throat, chest, and lower.

Feel this warmth and golden light spread through your body, making it soft and relaxed.

Enjoy this state and let it fill you completely.

7.   Reflect on Your True Nature:

Record this resourceful state and remember how it feels.

From this state, ask yourself what you want to do. Write down your answers.

8.   Understand and Support Your Inner Self:

Ask yourself who is inside you and connected with the instinct you recognise. Talk to this part of you.

Release any emotions that come up.

Ask, "How can I support you now? How can I support myself now?" Keep asking until you reach the true need.

If the need is for love, acceptance, or safety, give it to yourself in your inner world. Visualize and feel this part of you being loved and safe.

9.   Integrate with Higher Support:

Ask your higher self for support in this experience.

Allow all necessary processes to take place and integrate harmoniously within you.

Imagine your guides and guardian angels providing love and support, ensuring your inner needs are met.

By following these steps, you can heal past experiences, reclaim your energy, and create a supportive and harmonious inner environment that empowers you to move toward your goals.

This practice can be used whenever you find yourself in an emotionally charged situation. It will help you calm down, gain a new perspective, and support yourself effectively by addressing your thoughts, feelings, and bodily reactions.

I will repeat the steps:

Prepare Yourself:

- Find a quiet and comfortable place where you won't be disturbed.
- Sit down in a comfortable position.
- Close your eyes and take several deep breaths. Inhale deeply, hold for a moment, and then exhale slowly.
- Relax your face, forehead, shoulders, spine, arms, and legs.

1. Collect Your Thoughts:
- Place your hand on your head.
- Focus on the thoughts and beliefs you are experiencing in the current situation. What are you telling yourself? What are your immediate thoughts?
- Write down these thoughts without any corrections or judgments.

2. Collect Your Feelings:

- Move your hand to your heart, your chest.
- Bring up the emotions that your thoughts are evoking. Allow yourself to feel and acknowledge all your feelings.
- Write down these emotions honestly, without filtering.

3. Collect Your Bodily Reactions:
    Place your hand on your lower belly.

- Tune into what your body wants to do in this situation. Do you feel like running, fighting, freezing, fawning, disappearing, shouting, becoming small, avoiding confrontation, hiding, etc.?
- Feel these impulses and write them down.

4. Support Yourself:

- Hold your hand on your lower belly and speak to yourself:
- "Now I see it. I accept and admit my instinct to [name the instinct, e.g., run] and how it supports my safety."
- "I admit all my thoughts, feelings, and emotions. And right now, I admit that I do not have to [name the instinct] to feel safe! I choose my reality, where I can stay and do what I want to do. I choose the appropriate right action, and it will be safe for me!"
- Repeat these affirmations, ensuring they resonate deeply within you.

5. Reclaim Your Energy:

- Visualise the energy you spent on this strategy as a big cloud of light.
- Imagine reclaiming this energy back for a new strategy and new decisions.
- Let this energy fill your body, starting from your head and moving down to your shoulders, throat, chest, and lower.
- Feel this warmth and golden light spread through your body, making it soft and relaxed.
- Enjoy this state and let it fill you completely.

6. Reflect on Your True Nature:
- Record this resourceful state and remember how it feels.
- From this state, ask yourself what you want to do. Write down your answers.

7. Understand and Support Your Inner Self:
- Ask yourself who is inside you and connected with the instinct you recognise. Talk to this part of you.
- Release any emotions that come up.
- Ask, "How can I support you now? How can I support myself now?" Keep asking until you reach the true need.
- If the need is for love, acceptance, or safety, give it to yourself in your inner world. Visualize and feel this part of you being loved and safe.

8. Integrate with Higher Support:
- Ask your higher self for support in this experience.
- Allow all necessary processes to take place and integrate harmoniously within you.
- Imagine your guides and guardian angels providing love and support, ensuring your inner needs are met.

Benefits:

Calm Your Reptilian Brain: This practice helps calm your reptilian brain, which compels us to see threats where there are none.
- **Gain Perspective:** By calming down, you gain a different perspective on the situation.
- **Support Yourself:** This practice supports your mental, emotional, and physical well-being, helping you respond more effectively to challenging situations.

Thank yourself for your hard work. You are amazing, and you have just moved mountains inside you.

Practice 12:

Reflecting on your achievements is a powerful exercise in self-recognition and gratitude. Here's a way to guide yourself through this reflection:

1. Review Your Journey: Take some time to think about the various roles you've had and the milestones you've reached throughout your career. Consider both big and small achievements.

2. Acknowledge Your Efforts: Recognise the hard work, dedication, and perseverance that brought you to where you are. Reflect on the skills you've developed and the knowledge you've gained.

3. Celebrate Your Successes: Make a list of your accomplishments, both personal and professional. Celebrate the projects you've completed, the challenges you've overcome, and the goals you've met.

4. Express Gratitude: Thank yourself for the commitment and effort you've put into your work. Appreciate the times you've pushed through difficulties and the resilience you've shown.

5. Embrace Your Growth: Recognise how far you've come since the beginning of your career. Reflect on the growth and progress you've made over the years.

6. Look Forward: Think about how these experiences have prepared you for future opportunities. Embrace the confidence and competence you've built and let it inspire your next steps.

By doing this, you not only honour your past achievements but also empower yourself for continued growth and success.

Last Kind Reminder:

By setting and achieving your goals, you should never forget about your desires and interests outside your goals. If you consistently say no to something you want to do, for example, like draw or take a dance class, you say no to an essential part of yourself. The consequences might be losing meaning, getting tired, and becoming dissatisfied with what you do.

We call it life-work balance, which is paramount for our mental health.

By finding balance and thoughtfully integrating your interests, you can create a fulfilling and harmonious life.

Thank you for your time, your energy, your awareness and your desire to help yourself.

With total, absolute respect and love for you, my dear reader! We are all more alike and more connected than we can imagine.

It is my honour to be a brief part of your life through my book.

Humbly and sincerely yours,

Valeria.